Random Thoughts n' Lotsa Coffee

A Collection of Writings Inspired by Real Life.

Random Thoughts n' Lotsa Coffee

A Collection of Writings Inspired by Real Life.

By: J.V. Manning

Caffeinated Inspirations Publishing Co.

Caffeinated Inspirations Publishing Co.

Printed and bound in the United States

ISBN-13: 978-0615788036 (Caffeinated Inspirations Publishing Co.)

ISBN-10: 0615788033

Library of Congress Card Number – Pending
Random Thoughts n' Lotsa Coffee / J.V. Manning
ISBN 0615788033
1st Edition

Correspondence can be sent to:
J.V. Manning
Caffeinated Inspirations Publishing Co.
P.O. Box 602
Standish, ME 04084

email: thoughtsandcoffee@gmail.com

© J.V. Manning
www.randomthoughtsandlotsacoffee.com

Dedicated to:

Marnie. A woman who loved me without fail and taught me life lessons over our morning coffee.

May she forever be an angel on my shoulder.

&

My husband, Marc and son, Trey. Without their love, humor, and encouragement, none of this would have been possible.

Inspired Coffee Talk

I may not know where my road leads or what is around the next turn.
I may not see the sudden potholes or dark clouds gathering.
I do know that I will continue walking - overcoming all I find.
I will walk with humor and love. I will never lose my stride.

Life can be so random – on top of the world one moment, and lying on the ground in the next breath wondering what hit you. Life is filled with good times and bad, happiness and sadness, ups and downs and all arounds that can leave you filled with wonder or in tears. There is no rhyme or reason. You simply do the best you can with what you have, and continue on.

There are so many souls in this world who feel lost, so many who feel lonely even when surrounded by friends and family. There are many who feel like there is no one else in the world who understands them and that no one on this giant planet is facing what they are or trying to deal with the same emotions as they. They feel isolated.

Which is how Random Thoughts n' Lotsa Coffee came to be.

I was sitting at my kitchen table one day lost in thought and wondering in which direction to go. My life was a mess filled with drama, sadness, fear and devastating loss. I sat there lost in my thoughts when suddenly I had an overwhelming need to get it all out of me.

So, I made a fresh pot of coffee and on a whim, began to create Random Thoughts n' Lotsa Coffee. I created a website and blog, then a page on Facebook and – for no one else but me (or so I thought at the time) – began to write. It was probably one of the single most important turning points in my life and one that I never saw coming. I am humbled and so grateful to realize that within the past 2 years my musings on life, my experiences, my darkest moments and greatest triumphs, have reached thousands of souls all across the globe. To realize that others could benefit from my teachings and words is humbling and exciting. To bring it all together within this book – a dream come true.

My husband told me once that I was a leader who did not demand to be followed – that I allowed people to make their own decisions and choices in their lives, but was always there beside them when they needed me. I thought at the time how perfectly that summed me up. I make no demands on people. I do not tell them how to think, what to think or how they should feel. It is not my style. What I will do, as you will read in the following pages, is share the wisdom and the insight I have gained on my journey through life. I am no self-help guru. I hold no secret keys to happiness or strength. But in these pages, I will share with you different perspectives and ways to learn to love and respect yourself. I will show you that even without knowing, you have had the strength inside of you the whole time – I just help you remember.

Written from a place inside myself that I never knew existed but was so thrilled to have discovered, my words aren't always pretty, never flowery and tend to be pretty straightforward. I know, however, that they will resonate with you. I know that you will draw strength from these pages and go on about your life remembering that you are strong, you are human and you deserve to be happy. You will own your life – past, present and future. I know this because I too have walked such a long journey to get to where I am today. And I will keep on walking, facing life and all its lessons, and writing about them in the process.

I have always found that in times of great sadness, stress and life turmoil, the warmth of a hot cup of coffee gave me something to center myself with, something to hold on to that would warm me and fuel my random thoughts. *"A cup of coffee shared with a friend is happiness tasted and time well spent."* Welcome to my random world. May your coffee be hot, your thoughts be random and when you turn the final page, may you feel empowered, excited and strong.

J.V. Manning

Note to Self

There comes a point in life when you need to silence all the outside voices and only listen to yourself. You have to learn to listen to the voice of your soul, for it knows best what you need to hear, need to learn and need to know. Stop silencing it. That little voice is your instinct, your strength and the culmination of your life experiences.

Listen when your soul speaks...

Dear *Self,*

I need to talk to you. You won't hear me when I try to come through your dreams or when I pass random thoughts through your head during the day. There are some things I need you to hear, to appreciate and to get through your thick skull. I watch your daily struggles. I see you in the mornings getting ready for work and can hear your thoughts as you look in the mirror. I feel the pain as you bite your tongue over and over again failing to speak your mind and to stand up for yourself. I see you dealing with the past and I see your lack of trust in the future.

Self- You and I need to talk.

Stop second guessing yourself. Trust is something that is learned- I understand that. I know it is something you struggle with time after time. But if you can't learn to trust yourself, you will never learn to trust another. You need this lesson. You need to learn to trust. Same thing with letting people in. Keeping people at arm's length because you don't want them to have the power to hurt you- is hurting you. I know you have been hurt in the past. I have felt every betrayal and cried every tear with you. But holding the people in your life accountable for the actions of those who came before is simply not going to work anymore.

You are tired. I feel the heaviness in your step and the weight on your shoulders. Giving and receiving is a balance in life and if you keep giving and giving you will end up empty and of no use to anyone. Especially yourself. No one else is going to force you to step back and give yourself some time. It is not their job. It is yours and yours alone. Use your words. Asking for help is not a sign of weakness. It is a sign of maturity and gives the people in your life a chance to step up. They need this as much as you do.

You are not a robot. Emotions need to be felt fully and appreciated. Happiness is awesome but sometimes it just doesn't happen. You have been through hell and back over the past few years. Give yourself time to appreciate your journey. Give yourself time to heal. Understand that this doesn't make you weak. It makes you human. Understand Self that you will never break. You may bend at times or fall to your knees- but you will always, always pick yourself back up. This goes back to the learning to trust yourself lesson. Learn it.

You are not your past. You are not your history. You are your today and your future. Your life is not defined by where you come from, what you have faced or where you are going. It is defined by what you do in each moment. How you face your challenges, how you treat others and how you treat yourself. I know you have been hurt by the actions of people you cared about. Shit happens sometimes. We both know life ain't always pretty nor is it always easy. But it is worth it.

Taking care of everyone around you is admirable. But, you have got to take care of yourself too. Stop denying those nagging pains, doctor's appointments or massages you secretly crave but never splurge on. You work hard. You deserve it. See to it that you get what you need. Own your life and give to it what you so freely give to others. Stop being a damn martyr. You want something- then get off your butt and go for it. Expect no one to motivate you but yourself. Listen to yourself. Stop being your own worst enemy and just do it.

Self, we have been together since the beginning of time. Through heartbreaks and tears, triumphs and losses, I have always been proud of you. Proud of your accomplishments and proud of your failures for you never fail to see the lesson in them. Stop silencing me when I tell you these things. Hear me loud and clear. These negative thoughts of yours come from a voice that needs to be silenced once and for all. Silence it. For the both of us. It hurts our heart when I hear you put yourself down.

Remember all those years ago when you and I last had a heart - to - heart talk? It was a moment when you had let your defenses down and my voice came through. You heard me loud and clear before you shut me out. I am your instinct. I am the beat of your heart and the firing synapses in your mind. I am the culmination of everything you have worked so hard for. I am the tears you have cried, the smiles you have beamed and the faith that you have in yourself. Stop silencing me and believe. Believe in yourself. Trust your internal power and the sheer force of your soul. Stop playing small. Stop walking away and learn to fight for yourself. Know your worth. Know it from the depths of your soul. The world doesn't give it to you. Relationships don't give it to you. Nothing outside yourself is capable of defining your worth, only you. Stop selling yourself short and live out loud. Live authentically and live to the best of you. The world needs it. The world needs you and all you have to offer.

But first you must hear me when I talk to you. Whatever life brings for good or for worse- always believe in yourself. Stop silencing that little voice inside your soul. For that little voice is the champion of your existence and will never ever let you down.Believe in it and believe in yourself once and for all.

Thanks for finally listening.

Love,
   Yourself

A Leap of Faith

There is nothing to be gained in hiding behind your fear. There is nothing to be gained but wrapping yourself in guilt and sadness. And everything to be gained in releasing it so that you can take that leap of faith and build your wings on the way down. There is no shame in laughter, no shame in wanting to allow the light back in.

A few years back a friend gave me a bookmark. On it was a picture of an angel and the quote from Kobi Yamada; "Sometimes you need to take a leap of faith and build your wings on the way down." This quote that has stuck with me all these years. Usually popping into my head when I am in the process of talking myself out of doing or starting something that could potentially change my life.

Why are we more often our own worst enemy instead of our own very best friend?

Fear.

Fear of change, happiness, failure or whatever we can conjure up in our minds, which give us an excuse to put the brakes on life's possibilities. If we never take that step then we will never fall flat on our face. We fear the unknown and therefore block ourselves from learning something new before we even get started. We fear letting go of the past and moving on. So we block ourselves and get creative with excuses to justify it. Trying to convince not only the world but ourselves that it is the right decision to not take that leap.

But it is not just changing that so many are afraid of or trying new things. People fear life itself. They do not trust in it, in their happiness, their abilities or the future. They fear moving on from the past. They fear moving on from love lost, relationships that have ended, their grief or their memories. Simply because moving on from these things will lead them into the great unknown where they could get hurt again and open themselves up to feeling emotions that they long ago sealed off in self preservation. So they draw protective shields around themselves and plant their feet and shroud their life in sadness, grief, anger and frustrations- because these are the only things they trust and believe in.

You become a prisoner of your circumstance. Denying yourself the freedom of releasing it all and taking a leap of faith so that you can move on and be happy. Move on and allow the light back into your life. You say that you can't. That it is too soon or that you could never open yourself up to the chance. The chance of losing again or exposing yourself to the possibility of getting hurt. You allow the darkness of your fear to take over while holding the key to the chains that bind you the whole time. You are not helping yourself. You are not protecting yourself. You are only short changing yourself.

There is nothing to be gained in hiding behind your fear. There is nothing to be gained but wrapping yourself in guilt and sadness. And everything to be gained in releasing it so that you can take that leap of faith and build your wings on the way down. There is no shame in laughter, no shame in wanting to allow the light back in. There is no shame in saying your peace once and for all to what has hurt you, taken away your life and rendered you a shell of who you once were. By saying good bye to it and making peace once in for all with what has happened to you, you turn that key on the lock to the chains that bind you. You begin releasing your fear and you begin making that turn to the light.

The light of your tomorrow.

It is scary releasing your sadness and shrugging off your fear and moving forward. You believe in your sadness and trust in your fear because it feels right. The worst has happened and by not moving on from it, it can't happen again. You hold tight to your feelings of guilt and scoff that you could ever be happy. You have lost so much. It would be a disservice to the one that died. You cringe at the thought of loving again- once burned twice shy. You trust more in the bad that has happened then you ever could in the future of possibilities.

Seriously, enough.

Your relationship ended. Probably badly and you have more "love" wounds than you care to admit. Or you lost someone who you loved so much, whose death has rendered your heart empty. You will never smile or feel whole again, you say to yourself. And you won't if you keep stopping yourself.

Release it. Once and for all.

Allow the light back in to your life. Unlock the chains that bind you and LEAP! Release your fear of the unknown and make room in your heart and your life for happiness. Trust that while bad happens - good does too. Know how I know that? Because when you release the fear- You put good back into to the world by simply being a part of it.

Take that leap of faith and build your wings on the way down. You will fly before you know it.

Hitting Curve Balls

There are times in life when you either need to acclimate to changes that are out of your control and roll with it or just give up. I refuse to give up. I may get frustrated, sad or tired- but I will continue on. Quitting is never an option.

There are times in life when something completely out of your control comes out of the blue and knocks you off your feet. You are faced then with the decision- do you just sit there shaking your head at the unfairness of it or do you get up and figure out what you need to do?

It is in this moment that your whole life can be defined.

You can either acclimate to your new situation. Understanding that changes need to be made- you identify what you need to do in order to make it work. Allowing yourself moments of frustrations, fear and sadness, but not for too long. You need to have these feelings and use them to fuel you on. You will make what adjustments are needed in order to continue on with your life.

Or you quit. Retreat into the darkness and refuse to change, acclimate or fight to adjust to your new circumstances. You tell yourself you are not strong enough, tough enough or that is just isn't worth it. You allow your life to go on auto-pilot and just float through your days as a fallen leaf floats down a stream.

How you handle the curve balls of life not only defines you, it also defines the quality of your existence. Floating through life never touching shore, never planting your feet and never looking up at the sky shaking your fist and say "Aww hell no- I won't quit!" is taking the easy way out. Don't get me wrong here; floating can be very healing when you are in the immediate aftermath of a curve ball. Grief, illness, job loss or whatever your curve ball is, deserves real emotion and sometime to experience it. You have to experience your curve ball, let the emotions flow, and NOT hide them, bottle them up or deny them if you ever plan to get past them to the acclimating stage.

The key here is not the deny your fear or sadness with what has happened, but to let it come, let it happen and then let it flow past you as you get ready to begin life anew. It may not be the life that you envisioned, wanted or dreamed of, but it is what it is. And that "is" will only be what you make it.

Believe me when I say- I get it.

I feel like I have hit so many curve balls that I should quit my job and go play for the Red Sox. It is the out – of – the - blue; never – saw – it - coming ones that get me. Going along minding your own business and BAM! I have been tempted over the years to just swing and miss and take the out. But then I find some part of me that refuses to quit and it gives the rally cry and I dust myself off and get ready to come out swinging.

Like now for instance. A little known fact about me - I have junk legs. Since the time when I was 8 years old and my knees started dislocating and every day since, I have had some level of pain. I acclimated each time they would get worse and continue on. I knew I would never be able to run or jump like the other kids when I was younger or as I got older be as physically active as I would like. But I have always said- it is what it is. I won't let them stop me. Some days are worse than others and I have learned to ignore the pain and try and not let them dictate my life. It has been a long time since they forced me to stop completely and recalculate- until now. Bouncing back is not as easy as it was when I was younger. Now I have to worry about the possibility of not being able to walk for a period of time. I found myself on Sunday scared and exhausted and having a hard time wrapping my head around it. Then I remembered what I was made of. So I picked up my bat and prepared myself to knock this curve ball out of the park like all the rest. I will handle whatever life throws at me because I can. Because I refuse to quit or feel sorry for myself. Because like all of you - I have worked too hard to get to this point in my life.

This moment in time may very well change my existence. But I will acclimate. I may get frustrated, sad and tired, but I will continue on. As will you. Quitting is never an option.

Eggs, Bread and
A Pound of Wisdom

Have you ever noticed that life often has a way of bringing us messages when we need them most? Whatever form they take we never fail to see it as an instant truth we were meant to hear.
It is simply magic.

Life lessons are not always hard.

Sometimes life will drop some random knowledge on you that helps you to become a better person, a better parent or a better friend. A random life lesson that shows you something that you never considered before but once you hear it, find that it strongly resonates with your soul. Innately knowing that you stumbled upon a truth you needed to hear. A truth that you know must be adapted into your life and that you will be better for it. You never see these subtle life synchronicities until they stop you cold with the power of them.

The other night I was having a talk with my teenage step-son concerning the importance of always telling the truth and how essential it was to be able to trust him. He had made a poor decision, and while it wasn't all that major, it was something that needed to be addressed. He and I have some pretty intense and in-depth conversations that for all intents are pretty spectacular from the mom point of view. Probably not so much from the teenage boy's view for now, but hopefully the lessons will carry on with him into his adult years. We both are learning lessons as he grows up; and I find that he teaches me even as much I as hopefully teach him. He teaches me patience. He teaches me creativity and how to think outside of the box to help him with life lessons he is facing. Watching him grow and watching him absorb each thing life brings up continues to be such an awe-inspiring journey. He has taught me to reach to depths of myself that I didn't know existed, in order to be the best step mom I can be.

The next morning we headed out to do our Saturday errands, which meant a trip to the grocery store. He and I both sighed at the thought of fighting the crowd of shoppers getting ready for yet another Maine snowstorm. We decided to just head out early and hope to avoid the worst of the craziness.

It was a shopping trip that I will remember forever.

As we made our way around the produce section we were bantering back and forth. Playfully giving each other a hard time as we tried to get some enjoyment out of such a mundane task. More often than not we get people laughing in the aisles with our antics which both of us enjoy immensely. Stopping in the first aisle to browse salad dressings I looked as an elderly lady came up behind us. I could hear her chuckle to herself as I pretended to give my kid a hard time about being too lazy to bend over and grab something off the shelf. As she made her way around me she reached out and patted my shoulder and looked up at me with a sparkle in her eyes. "He is learning every day. He will get it don't you worry. You just have to have patience and be thankful he wasn't a girl. They are harder," she said to me with a grin as she turned her attention to him. "You will get there son, work hard, be honest and grow up to be a good solid man. You must always be truthful." With these two gems of wisdom she went shuffling off leaving us staring at each other wondering what had just happened. I winked at his stunned expression and we carried on with our shopping. Turning down the next aisle there was yet another elderly woman standing there. Honestly it seemed like she must have been waiting for us- for as soon as we turned into the aisle- she looked at my kid and without provocation laid some "gray haired wisdom" down on him; "Son you will get there. You will figure it all out. Don't you worry. Sometimes lessons can be hard to take. I know growing up is hard but it is worth it. Just remember to always do what is right." As she walked away down the aisle she turned back to me and reminded me to always have patience. He will figure things out in time.

As we stood there and watched her walk away, I turned to the kid and remarked that apparently life lessons were on sale today. He regarded me with the best teenage boy face he could muster and said it felt like Marnie *(our beloved grandmother)* was using these elderly ladies to teach him a lesson from heaven. With a grin he glanced up and said "I got it already" which made me laugh right out loud as we continued our shopping and bantering. The next aisle was clear of wise old crones and I could see the relief on his face as he made it to the end. We made it half way up the next aisle before it happened again. Surprise blitz attack from a shopping grandmother and more pearls of wisdom for the kid and for me as well. This lady made sure to tell him to "Trust that everything works out and you will get to where you need to be. Remember to always listen, pay attention and work hard for what you want. Always be honest and listen to your mother." Looking me square in the eye she said to understand he will try my patience and push buttons I didn't even know I had, but to be strong and continue teaching him all that I could. He would get it eventually, rest assured. Off she went with a little old lady chuckle and a good shaking of her pointer finger at the both of us.

The remainder of our shopping was free of wisdom - bearing grannies but I could see the effect that they had on the kid. Though keeping an eye out for more grandmothers he was lost in his thoughts, as was I. He looked at me at one point and said; "who knew you could get eggs, bread and wisdom at a grocery store?"

Who knew?

Life often has a way of bringing us messages when we need them most. From stumbling upon a powerful quote that touches your soul, dialogue between characters on a TV show that hits home or a song playing on the radio that puts words to your jumbled thoughts. We must pay attention as we go through our daily moments to what others are trying to teach us whether they know they are inspiring us or not. You can feel it when it happens, that tingling in your belly and that feeling in the back of your neck that you were supposed to hear this particular truth. It serves as a reminder that magic is everywhere and we are not all alone on our journeys. We are a part of something so much bigger than ourselves and it is amazing.

Just watch out for those little old ladies at the grocery store. They got some zingers.

Our Own Worst Enemy

Look in the mirror and stop finding flaws.
Stop bullying yourself and start appreciating everything you are.
Because you know what?
Everything you are right this moment is perfect.
It is perfect because it is YOU.

I was sitting in a local coffee shop recently drinking my coffee and trying to write. I spent more time looking out the window. The weather outside appeared to have cleared and the snow that had been falling had finally stopped. The parking lot though plowed, still had piles of snow and a thick sheet of ice covering it. Maine in the wintertime is beautiful but it is also a pain in the ass sometimes. I watched as a SUV pulled in and parked. Slowly each of the doors opened and 4 well dressed women got out of the vehicle all of them frantically clutching the door to keep from falling. Slowly they made their way to the back of the vehicle while holding an over sized purse in one hand and the side of the SUV with the other. I had to stifle a chuckle, as I noticed that they were all wearing very expensive boots with 6 - inch heels.   Eventually they ran out of vehicle to hold onto and began to grasp one another as they made their way across the icy lot. I could hardly control my laughter watching the panicked looks on their faces as they made their way inside. Who wears 6 - inch heels in a snowstorm? Who forgoes the L.L. Bean boots for their Aldos in a Maine snow storm? Apparently, these women.

I just as quickly lost interest as they entered in a whirl of expensive perfume, giggling and orders of extra skinny this with half cafe whatever. Honestly their orders gave me a headache so I went back to my laptop and tried to get something going. Of course the troupe of the high-heeled women sat directly behind me. Their conversation never missing a beat as they removed their jackets and sat down. Much to my chagrin I found that instead of tuning them out I eavesdropped on their conversation. I couldn't help myself.

Each one of these women was beautiful by society's standards. Slim, perfect hair and makeup and dressed to the nines for a simple coffee date. Yet for the next hour each one of them went on and on about everything that was wrong with them. From diets they were trying, to their hours with a trainer and on to comparing themselves to famous celebrities and what they would give to have someone else's body, hair or perfect teeth. They sat there and disparaged themselves more in that hour that I had in an entire week. These women weren't fishing for compliments from their friends either. They really believed what they were saying. That they were so flawed that they couldn't look in the mirror, stand on their scale or allow themselves to eat a slice of the chocolate cake that was taunting them from the counter. All for what? The quest to be perfect? I was stunned quite frankly. Here were 4 women who from the outside looking in lead perfect well coiffed lives and they hated themselves. Listening to them broke my heart and made me want to get them that cake.

I lost all interest in the piece I was writing and focused instead on what they were saying. The level of intensity that each one of these women hated themselves shocked me, saddened me and made me want to diet. Two of them were married as they referenced their husbands, one was dating and the last one in her words; "Will never find any man that would love her because of how gross she was." Her words not mine. This "gross" single lady was beautiful and every hetero guy with a pulse I know would agree. I wanted to hug her and then shake some sense into her.

Why couldn't she see what I saw?

Long after I left that coffee shop these women plagued my thoughts. I thought about all the negative thoughts I had on a daily basis. Thoughts that if someone outside of myself said to me I would probably punch in the nose. For the next week I found myself observing other women and listening to their conversations. Not once did I hear one of them say that they were proud or happy with themselves. Instead what I heard over and over was how every single one of them wanted to change into something prettier, skinnier or just all together different then what they were. How they would only be content when they looked like someone else. It made me sad and it made me angry to realize just how focused we are on changing the very things that make us unique. That we all feel we need to change what we look like in order to be *"just like everyone else"*.

Who sets these damn standards anyway?

I will tell you - we do.

We are our own worst enemies and we need to stop battling ourselves in the quest for perfection. From teenage girls to grown women the battle wages every day to be beautiful. Eating disorders rage out of control, depression and self hatred are the norm. We talk about bullying all the time and the devastating effect it has on the victims. But what about bullying ourselves? We bully ourselves every day, we disrespect ourselves and we belittle ourselves. It is not motivating; nor is it a kick in the ass to be a better person. It is simply convincing us that we are less than perfect and in this, not good enough. It has to stop. Who cares about society's standards or airbrushed models in magazines?

Look in the mirror and stop finding flaws. Stop bullying yourself and start appreciating everything you are. Because you know what? Everything you are right this moment is perfect. It is perfect because it is YOU. Having goals to work towards for personal betterment is one thing and always striving to be the best you possible is awesome. But love yourself in the process. Be who you are, extra pounds, wrinkles or out of control hair. Who cares? Before anyone else will love you- you must first love yourself.

Accept yourself flaws and all.

Sticks and Stones

One of the hardest lessons in life is knowing when to walk away.
To cut the ties that bind us to people we love.
But love should never hurt.
Love should never leave you feeling empty and alone and worthless.
Value yourself enough to know this and know that you can walk away.
You can silence the voices and move on.

Hurtful words will echo in your mind long after the voice that speaks them is silent. Like a record with a scratch repeating the words over and over, so do the words that cut us greater than any knife could. Even if the words are spoken in anger or as an off the cuff remark you feel them. You hear them and you worry them over in your mind until there comes a point that you start to believe them. If they came from someone you love, you respect and you cherish, well more often than not you incorporate them into your very being. As the ones who love us never wish to hurt us, right? But what if in the moment these words were spoken that is the very thing they wanted most?

Sometimes the people we love will say or doing something that hurts our feelings. That breaks our hearts and makes us second guess everything we believe about ourselves, for it is only those closest to us that hold that power. They hold that power though not by simply being family, spouse or friend. They hold that power because we give it to them. We give it to them with the belief that they will always use it to build us up when we stumble, build our confidence when it shakes and to always reaffirm that we are in fact loved and cherished. And sometimes that is exactly what they do. But sometimes the one we love will take that power so freely entrusted to them and use it not to build you up but instead use it to bring you down.

A childhood friend of mine had a father who would constantly berate her. Tell her she was worthless and would amount to nothing. That she was fat and ugly and no man would ever want her. She strove for excellence in everything she did to prove her worth. She won awards, she got amazing grades and she was a warm and caring person. She was a daughter to be proud of. Except he never was. And over the years his hurtful words and actions broke her. She stopped caring. She believed everything he ever told her. Things no parent should ever say to their child. She carried his words all through her life. She formed friendships but always kept them at arm length. She rarely dated and felt completely unworthy of attention. She was never good enough she believed, because her father had said so. Until one day she decided to take her power back. She took away his power to hurt her by simply walking away from him.

One of the hardest things in life is to know when it is time to walk away. We all have different thresholds to what we will tolerate from those closest to us. Family, spouses or friends are a part of our lives because we want them there. But what do you do when someone you care about hurts you over and over again? How many chances do you give someone until you throw your hands up and say no more? Personally I have mastered the art of walking away. Part of me is proud of the fact that I will not tolerate being hurt repeatedly, lied to or disrespected over and over by any one. Another part of me wonders if maybe I walk away too easily. It is the age old battle of mind versus heart in these matters and it is a battle all of us face at one time or another.

When is enough- enough?

I am all for second chances in most cases. We all make mistakes. But if someone you care about hurts you over and over again, chances are it is not by mistake. Like the saying goes, *"Fool me once shame on you. Fool me twice, shame on me."* We shouldn't continually sacrifice ourselves for anybody, yet we do. Over and over again. We tolerate being hurt by the very people that should never hurt us. Parents, spouses, family members or friends should not get a pass just because of who they are.

Words have the power to hurt you only as long as you allow it. I don't care if you share DNA with the one that spoke them or not. You do not need anyone to validate you except for the one person that knows you better than anyone- yourself. Take your power back from those that use it to hurt you and use it instead to fuel you on. Never let anyone make you second guess something you know in your heart is true. Trust and Value Yourself.

One of the hardest lessons in life is knowing when to walk away. To cut the ties that bind us to people we love. But love should never hurt. Love should never leave you feeling empty and alone and worthless. Value yourself enough to know this and know that you can walk away. You can silence the voices and move on. **You are worth it.**

Someday...

"Someday" doesn't exist, never has, and never will.
There is no "someday". There's only today.
When tomorrow comes, it will be another today;
so will the next day. They all will.
There is never anything but today.

Have you ever counted the times you say the words "someday" during the course of a week? Probably not, as we are all to busy worrying about it, planning for it, working towards it, that we actually forget, it doesn't really exist. Someday I will make enough money to buy her a ring, some day I will take a day off and go on an adventure, someday I will be happy when I... After I... Someday I will have time. But if some day doesn't exist, that means it never comes. So all the hard work and all the planning is for what? Someday is the ultimate procrastination. All of us are guilty of it, we do it every day and half the times don't even realize it. We are so caught up in work and the daily grind that we lose sight of what we have right now. We have today. If you can't see beyond what you think you are working towards, saving for, how will you know when you are there? Rarely do we stop and say- Today is my Someday. Today I am going to make it happen. I am going to tell the person I am with that I love them; I am going to take my kids to get ice cream instead of spending more hours at work. I am going to make my wife put on her fancy clothes *(that probably still have the price tags attached)* and take her on a date. Today, instead of traveling the never ending road to Someday, I am actually going to arrive.

The way to get started is to quit talking and begin doing. I mean seriously do we actually think that the world will end if we take the time? Are the planets going to collide and stars fall from the sky? Will our employers have to close the doors because we decided that for one moment in time, we were going to live our someday? Probably not, but to us when faced with this, will fall back on any excuse we can think of as to why it's impossible. What we don't understand is that there is always, "something" and maybe that something can wait until someday to get done.

And its not just events we put off. Its decisions and changes and life. We stay in situations and hope that someday things will be different, some day she will change, some day he will understand me. Someday I will go after that job, that degree, that guy. Some day I will speak my mind. Someday I will write again..*(Yeah that was mine)* and then its not procrastination, its plain ole fear. Fear of failure, of rejection, sometimes fears of success. Because once we get there and we do it, we have no idea what to do next, and that scares us. Thus the cycle continues, and it is a circle of some days.

We all need to man up. We all need to take stock of what is important to ourselves, our families, our lovers and friends and stop living on the fantasy island called Someday I'll...

Can you do it?

Burning Bridges

*I can't sleep at night, I toss and I turn, I keep losing sight of the lessons
I've learned I'm standing at the crossroads with just one concern.
Which bridge to cross and which bridge to burn I need to
reach a decision.
And get on with the rest of my life.*
~ Vince Gill

At one point in our lives we have all been faced with this decision - do you leave the bridge standing, do you cross it and never look back or do you burn that bridge and all that it represents and forge a new path of your life? Do you even cross that bridge? That bridge over the course of your lives could represent any number of life's lessons. Bad relationships, jobs, toxic friendships, life's status quo. At one point you find yourself in a situation where you have to either cross that bridge and start a new chapter, choose a different path and leave it standing just in case or cross the bridge and burn it with the finality of never ever going back.

This is one of the hardest life lessons we are faced with. Which bridge to cross and which bridge to burn. If we walk away from a situation in our lives and leave that bridge standing, it allows ourselves the option of returning to what it was the drove us away in the first place. We can always go back if crossing this bridge didn't work out. Kind of a safety net to catch us if we fail. Sometimes this is ok to leave that option open, but when is it not? When is it time to torch that bridge to our past? When do we finally decide that enough is enough and we will never go back? Back to a certain person or situation that drove us across the bridge in the first place. How many times do we get right up to the entrance of that bridge and panic or second guess ourselves and turn around, never even taking that first step?

What is the driving force behind us that even gets us to this point? How do you know when enough is enough and it is time to move on, no more second, third, fifty chances. That internal struggle is different for each of us, but the same too. We all battle the same question- when is it time to walk away? We never really want to give up on someone, or something in our lives, but there comes a time when we really do not have a choice. It's not healthy for us to stay, we are unhappy or unfulfilled, we begin to refuse to sacrifice ourselves and stand up for what we need.

Over the years I have faced my own share of bridges. Some I have crossed and left standing because maybe at that particular time something minor wasn't right for me, but maybe after some time had passed, I would like to be able to return. I made the decision to walk away based on feelings or where I was in my life at the time. This is usually the case, but there have been a couple that I have decided needed to be burned to the ground. Usually the ones that I have burned have been to people who were too toxic to want in my life any more. I had gotten to that point of no return, where I had tried and tried to make things work and had failed. It takes a lot to get me personally to this point, but it happens and I am ok with that. What I had to figure out though was- when was enough-enough?

Is there ever really a solid point when you realize that you can't do it anymore? Does it build up and build up until that proverbial straw breaks your back? Is it one event that opens your eyes and asks- What are you still doing here? Honestly I have had both. That lighting bolt from my subconscious that said- The time to move on is now! Other times it has be gradually over time and once it took me 30 years to figure out. I guess it depends on the person or situation. Nothing in life is black and white, there are always shades of gray and in those shades of gray is our life. It is the balance between doing what is right and what is right for us. Therein lies the lesson that life is teaching us. We can't always do what is right for others; we must come to a point where we do what is right for ourselves. Burn down that bridge and move on. Others in your life may not get it or understand and that's ok, you can explain to them or not. I usually say that I needed to honor my self, my life and made the decision to stay or go based on that.

While people may not understand, if they love you they should respect it.

Burning Bridges is something at one point we all must do in our lifetime, usually more than once. We all have the strength inside of us to make this decision, to know when to walk away, what we just need to realize is that it is ok. Staying true to yourself is so important that sacrificing it to a job you hate, a bad relationship or family member that crosses the line is never really an option for long without losing that one thing that is so worth fight for, starting over for - **You.**

Love Me or Hate Me

A competent and self-confident person is incapable of jealousy in anything. Jealousy is invariably a symptom of neurotic insecurity.
~ Robert A. Heinlein

I live my life being true to one thing, myself. My actions, beliefs and thoughts are no one's but my own. I live what is right for me, how I want to live, feel and be. If people don't like that, well that's fine with me, to each their own. I am who I am, take it or leave it. I work hard for what I have, went through a lot of bad relationships to get to the perfect one, I stand up for myself and others, am up front and honest with everyone, and I am happy. I know who I am, what I am capable of, what my strengths and weaknesses are and how far I will go for my friends and family. I am here to please no one but myself and those I love. To me this is living life honestly. I am who I am. How else would someone that is well adjusted, confident and strong be? And why does this incite such hostility and jealousy in certain types of people? I call them the neurotics. People who allow their insecurities to fuel their daily lives. That sees someone who is happy and decides that because they are not happy in their own lives, it is their duty to try and destroy, ruin and change another's happiness.

I have such a hard time fathoming why the neurotics seem to think that this makes for a happy life. Jealousy is a nasty green little creature that if allowed, will control all of your thoughts and actions that to me could be better spent improving your own life. Typically when this behavior arises in someone who I am somehow connected with, I will simply ignore it. Their insecurities can have no bearing on how I live my life. However, when it doesn't end there, and it starts to affect me personally, I get really cranky. Why should I have to alter my life, how I am, in order to justify their issues? If it happens to be someone close to me, then I will take the time to understand the motivation behind their actions. I may try and talk to them about it. Probably though I will just ignore it, until it directly effects me. By directly affecting me, I mean when it goes beyond the line of simple jealousy that we all have been at one time or another in our lives. Our best friends get an awesome job or new car. One of our buddies has a hot new girlfriend while you are still searching for the perfect one. These are normal jealous feelings that disappear just as fast as they arise. It's when the person who is jealous takes it that step further and tries to ruin the new relationship or stops being your friend because you have more than they and they just can't get over it. It's that line when crossed that gets me every time. When does it go from being happy for your friend to now you are the bad guy for being happy or successful?

And when did it become ok to sabotage the other person? Why must people who allow their jealousy to control them, have the right to try and destroy what makes us happy? And why does it always seem to be, that when we stand up for ourselves and call them on it, we end up the bad guys? Or don't call them on it and just let them go, not feeding into their drama, so they step it up a notch in order to get our attention, in order to hurt us as they feel we have hurt them? Why is it a never - ending battle? When did it become not ok to be happy, loved and successful?

How do you stop the other person's issues from affecting you? Especially if it is a situation from which you really can't extract yourself from? How do you while staying true to yourself say- Hey! Knock this shit off! Enough already. Instead of trying to destroy what you don't have, or what you envy in another, why not turn that energy inside and fix what you have broken inside of you? How do you get this person to understand, that while their actions may hurt you now, in the long run it is totally themselves that will pay the price?

It can be hard not to react to it, not to allow their actions to change how you are. Especially if they are constantly running their mouth off about you with lies and manipulating those around you to also believe their fantasy. Because often times that is exactly how the little green monster rears its ugly head- in lies and stories that have no basis in anything other than someone's neurotic insecurities. I guess the question is do you even justify it with a response? Do you let it go? Or do you confront it head on? I have tried personally all of the above and have come to the conclusion there really is only one way to react. Continue to live your life. Continue to trust in yourself and who you are. Tune out the neurotics and their tales and drama. Live your life as you are, doing what makes you happy. They will either get over it or not. In the end, the truth is, it's not really your problem. It is totally their own. Until they turn their thoughts inside and look at themselves they will never be happy or confident.

Never, ever change who you are, for someone else's insecurities. Stay true to the one person in this world you need to worry about - yourself.

Define Yourself

We either make ourselves miserable or we make ourselves strong.
The amount of work is the same.
~Carlos Castaneda

How many of us live in the day - to - day rut of just getting by? Not just financially, but emotionally as well. How many times a day does the frustration or sadness blip onto your internal radar, only to be pushed back down cause work is calling, or the kids need something or there is errands to be run and bills to be paid? So caught up in our daily lives that we never take the time to pull out those feelings and examine them. We continually push them down further and further and hope they stay there. Plaster that smile on and keep going. Until that one moment in time, when the planets collide and all of emotional crap we have been burying and burying comes flying out. Sometimes it is the smallest thing that sets us off, but it gives tell to just exactly unhappy, unfulfilled or how deep in a rut we really are. Who you are as a person will dictate how you handle it when it all comes to the surface. Will you bow your head and let the weight of the world drive you to your knees, will you hide out in bed and sleep, will you let your anger get the best of you and take it out on the ones you love? Will you over eat to fill the void or drink to dull the pain. Or will you pull your shoulders back and identify what exactly is causing your sadness, frustration and grab it by the balls and say, "OK! Listen up; here is what I am going to do."

I want to be the kind of person, who squares my shoulders back and says to myself - I got this.

I have done it more than once, as I am sure some of you have too. You just get to a point in your life, that you either gotta jump and hope for a solid landing, or stay where you are and lose all sense of yourself. It is never an easy thing, identifying all that is wrong in your life and really looking at it, not glossing it over, but see it for what it is. It takes the exact same amount of energy to make your life what you want it to be, to be happy, and to hold your head up, that it does to be miserable and unhappy. Why this is so hard for people confuses me. Why would you not want to be happy? Why does being happy scare us so? Why can we never trust in it?

I know that often times, the feelings of being trapped, selfish or weak take over. I had a lady one time say to me that, *"You are like a cup. If you are empty, then how will you quench another's thirst? You must first fill yourself, before you will be any good to another."* This is so true. I mean how are you supposed to be everything to everyone, if you aren't being everything to yourself first? This is really not a gender thing at all either; men and women both are guilty of it. We will travel the path in front of us that is the easiest; will not the most fulfilling, because we don't trust ourselves to make our own path. We don't trust that while our conscience thoughts may have no idea what the hell we are doing, our subconscious does. We know without really knowing until that time when it all comes to the surface and we make that decision. That decision will be a direct reflection of who you are. Are you stronger then you give yourself credit for? Are you brave enough to take that first glance at your life, and stop playing the victim, stop blaming the world for your unhappiness and then, only then can you begin to - define yourself.

I Have Learned

The best day of your life is the one on which you decide your life is your own. No apologies or excuses. No one to lean on, rely on, or blame. The gift is yours - it is an amazing journey. You alone are responsible for the quality of it. This is the day your life really begins
~Bob Moawad

Everyone feels emotional pain in their lives. You can either use that to become a better and stronger person or you use it as an excuse not to. I have learned over the years that there are times when a person will use it as an excuse. An excuse to retreat to some shadow world, where they refuse to deal with life and circumstance. Often times creating such a world that has no basis in reality, but is one that they are comfortable with. I have learned that sometimes, you can't fix broken.

I have learned that sometimes you cannot help someone that refuses to help themselves. That you can sacrifice for, plead with, fight for and love, and that sometimes, it isn't enough. I have learned that to carry the burden of this can almost bring you to your knees. I have learned that trying to show someone that the shadow world they live in is not reality, will never work. That a person so buried in this world will do whatever it takes to convince you, that it is you that is wrong. By lying, manipulating and swearing to whatever god is handy, you must agree and play along. To do otherwise marks you as the enemy. I have learned that sometimes, you can't fix broken.

I have learned what it is like to walk the edges of this shadow world, desperately wanting to reach in and bring this person back into life, to feel that constant pull from them as they resist. They want to pull you in, have you as part of this reality they have built. I have learned in this struggle the importance of strength. I have learned that to resist that pull, is to have a pull on your heart that is tremendous. I have also learned that you would come to a point, when you could pull no longer. I learned that sometimes, you can't fix broken.

I have learned over the years a lesson that seems to be coming to its final conclusion. That regardless of how much you love someone, support them and fight for them, they are ultimately responsible for their life, their journey, their reality. I have learned what it is like to fail. I have learned that sometimes you can't fix broken.

I have learned that while sometimes you can't fix broken, you can pick up the pieces of yourself and put them back together. This takes strength and courage. I have learned that when you decide your life is your own, that is the first step in taking back the power over your life. I have learned that this is ok. I have learned that you sometimes need to walk away.

Life lessons never stop, they just vary in intensity. How you handle life what throws at you, determines who you are as a person. I have seen the dangers of retreating into a shadow world; I have seen how high the cost can be when one will not fight for themselves. When it is simply just easier to retreat into their shadow world and leave their loved ones behind. I have learned, that it is never your fault, that they alone are responsible for their destiny.

I have learned that you alone are responsible for your character, your integrity, your strength and your future. I have learned that you must always dig as deep as you need to, to find the strength to pull yourself up and carry on. I have learned that the price is simply too high to not to. I have learned that it doesn't matter what the world thinks of you, if you are solid and secure in yourself, if you face whatever comes at you with dignity, strength and courage that is what matters. I have learned that it is ok to stumble; it is ok to cry, but that it must not end there.

I have learned the value of my life.

A Little Bit Stronger

I know my heart will never be the same. But I'm telling myself I'll be okay. Even on my weakest days. I get a little bit stronger
~Sarah Evans

The past week of my life has been one of the hardest I have ever had to live through, and that is saying something. I don't do feelings well, never have. I hate the thought circle that seems to be on constant rotation inside of my head while I work to process what has occurred. I am strong; have to be to get to be the person I am today. Hasn't ever been easy, but it is what it is, and I am who I am because of it. This event shattered my heart, made me angry and sad and a whole slew of other emotions that have my thoughts scattered. One of those moments in one's life that time seems to stop until you can wrap your head around it. I am not gonna lie, having a hard time with that. I feel like I am on a roller coaster and really wish it would stop so I could get my bearings. Life is like that at times, sending you screeching around curves with sudden drops that leave you breathless. You may get slightly off balance for a while, sometimes a little longer, but you get your feet back underneath you eventually. If you don't, the ride will go on without you and you will be left behind. Riding this roller coaster of life takes determination, takes balls, and takes integrity and strength. You have to want it, the ups, downs, curves and plummeting drops. To stop and get off means that you will never ride out of the past. The roller coaster of life goes only in one direction - forward. Sometimes you may need to take a break, to get your bearings and assess where you are, if it isn't where you want to be, you have to dig deep and fight to get where you want to be. People will weigh in; some will pass judgments on situations they have no idea about. But you can't listen to anyone but yourself. You have to want to fight when you have to, to see everything as it is, and get back on that ride. Always moving forward.

This is one of those times when I just wanted to yell, *"Stop the Frigging Ride, I want to get OFF!"* And I have, in a sense, taken a time out. This is ok, I know that. I need to let every emotion come as it will, face it and let it move on. Bottling it up isn't going to work, never has for me. I have to face it; all of it or else risk sacrificing the one thing that I have to fight for, me. No one else in my life has ever gone to bat for me, stuck up for me. I learned at an early age, that I had to be my own hero. Some people just don't understand and are so quick to judge, and that's fine. I let them.

Think about that for a minute, just letting people think what they want and not letting it hurt you. Because the only person for whom the truth is the most important is yourself. You have to live with what you have inside. You have to face it, or you risk losing yourself. We have to stop living for everyone else; we have to live for the one person in this life that should never, ever let you down, you.

You are the strongest person you know, even when you don't feel it. Family and friends can remind you when you are weak; they can give you all the love that you deserve. But there are times when life throws something at you, that you have to go inside yourself to find the answers. You will realize when this occurs, that while your world may be in pieces and the future may have suddenly taken a different shape, each piece you put back together will lead you to it. I know that this time, it may take me longer then usual to put the pieces back together. To make peace with what has occurred. Thankfully, I have a husband who reminds me everyday that I am strong, a kid that lights up my life and friends who are my family. While I may be alone in the processing of this, they are right behind me and for that I am grateful.

It is in your darkest hour of adversity, that you discover who you are and where you are meant to be. It is in this hour, that you learn more about yourself then you ever knew before. Who you will become, will depend on what you do when you are faced with it. Will you hide, will you run, will you be strong, will you become better for what has occurred? That is completely and utterly something only you can answer. For me, even on my darkest day, I will get a little bit stronger, I will continue forward after a time, because that is the only option I will allow myself. I hope for you, that it is the same. Never give up, life is too precious. It is totally what you make it, how you shape it, how you live it. You have total control even when at times it all feels like it is spiraling out of control. You have to fight at times, crawl at times, bow your head in weariness, but ultimately, you have to pick yourself up and tell yourself you will be ok. I wish for you strength, courage, and the ability to believe in yourself.

Random Thoughts in Progress

The thoughts that come often unsought, and, as it were, drop into the
mind, are commonly the most valuable of any we have.
~John Locke, 16 May 1699

Do you ever make time for silence? Moments in your day where you turn off your phones, computers, no radios, no conversation- nothing but silence. Moments where you shut off the world and let your mind wander where it will. Granted somedays, ok most days even finding five minutes to do this is next to impossible, or so we tell ourselves. Who has time? When actually the correct question would be, Who Doesn't Have Time? Often we all get so wrapped up in our days between work, kids, and marriages that we don't take a single moment for ourselves. To do so would make us feel guilty. Then there are those who cannot handle the silence. To be alone with one's thoughts can be almost intimidating to some. These are the people who from the time they wake up to the time they fall into bed exhausted, fill every moment of their day. People who are constantly busy, running, talking, doing, doing anything to avoid spending time with their thoughts. Each of us at one point or another is guilty of this. It's how long we let it go that determines what kind of life we will live. If you don't let your thoughts go, if you keep them under lock and key, how do you know if that sudden epiphany that would help you so much, is there or not?

Don't get me wrong, there are a lot of us *(raising my hand here)* who have a tendency to over think at times. To get this circle of thought into my head that goes around and around. I tend not to give it time to work out on its own. One of the lessons I have learned as I have gotten older is that sometimes there are problems or feelings in life that actually do not have a solution. Shocking I know, and most people will tell you that's wrong, but I believe there are circumstances that you will come across where you can think all you want and never be able to figure it out. It is what it is and that is all you have. Going in cirlces thinking about it does nothing but drive you crazy. I have often wished that we as humans came with an "off" switch on our thoughts; of course it would be far too easy to just flip the switch and never spend any time with ourselves.

What I want to figure out is the balance. The balance of allowing my thoughts to run free and not allowing them to go in circles at the same time. I feel that this is a fight we all have isn't it? We are human after all, though most days I will argue that I am in fact superhuman and can handle anything. Of course reality will often strike just as quickly and I get my reality check.

I do have to say that I love the moments of silence that I can steal in my day. Where I can turn everything off and let my mind go where it will. It is often in these moments when I do not focus on anything, interal or external that I will have a random thought drop from out of nowhere and it will be exactly what I needed. I just needed to give it the silence to come through. And while it may not be an answer that I have been searching for or expecting, it may be an alternative view or alternative thought that sheds a whole new light on whatever it is that is plaguing my thoughts.

So tell me, will you take ten minutes or even five minutes of silence? Will you let your mind wander untethered and see what comes through? Random Thoughts can be pretty amazing.

Shhhhh, let them come.

Moral Indignation is Jealousy with a Halo

The true hypocrite is the one who ceases to perceive his deception, the one who lies with sincerity.
~André Gide

There is no escaping them. At one point or another in our lives we have all had to deal with one of the hardest types of people to face, the hypocrite. I can tell immediately just from reading the first couple of sentences of this, you thought of someone, maybe if you are really lucky a couple, *(please note dripping sarcasm here)*. They appear sometimes out of no where, and usually we are completely unprepared to deal with them. Mainly because, if you are like me, you are who you are, always. You don't pretend to be something you are not, nor have ever been. The hypocrites almost seem not to be able to control themselves, so full of moral indignation they stand in judgement of everyone, except the one they should most be focusing on, themselves. They truly are toxic people, so wrapped up in the lives of others; they lose all touch with themselves. It is sad really, that they can stand in judgement of people, that which in truth, they probably know less then nothing about and proclaim, that they are right, that their beliefs are right, and you, just for being you, are wrong. I mean seriously, what the hell?

Now I know you are sitting there, reading this and probably grinning in contempt, because in your mind you have conjured the picture of your hypocrite. I call this person yours because I have my own and really do not need another. The hypocrite's crime is bearing false witness against themselves. What makes it so plausible to assume that hypocrisy is the vice of vices is that integrity can indeed exist under the cover of all other vices except this one. There is no honest hypocrite, I mean seriously think about it. Often times they lie first to themselves then to anyone that will listen, believing in their deceptions to the point it controls and skewers their perception of reality.

It really is the vice of all vices, isn't it? Honestly being in the presence of a hypocrite, or having the pleasure of hearing from them *(again note sarcasm)* makes me ultimately, feel a whole lot better about myself. I mean sure, it may sting at first, but becomes kinda like a reality check for yourself. You look within; assess the things the hypocrite is saying, and then smile. Because you have looked, you have measured yourself, and then moved on. Well hopefully moved on, but alas sometimes it is easier said than done, as we all know the hypocrite has a tendency to pick and pick and pick, each time getting more and more creative as to why they are right and you are wrong.

I know there are times when you get can't get away from them for one reason or another, so what do you do? Personally, I use these people as a sort of moral compass. While they judge me - I judge myself. And as I am my own harshest judge, as it is I that has to live with myself. As long as I like what I see, change what I don't, and continue on true to myself, then I know I am ok.

Because I know the reality of the situation is this...

The darkness that a hypocrite sees in another's heart - is simply just a reflection of what is in their own.

Life's Ambiance

*Enjoy the little things, for one day you may look back and
realize they were the big things.*
~Robert Brault

I am sitting here this evening at my kitchen table, writing on my laptop. I have a nice PC downstairs with a comfy chair and big desk, but I like being upstairs in the kitchen for some reason. I do my best writing here. I was pausing for a moment lost in thought, when I started looking around my home, started listening to the going - ons in the living room where my husband and stepson are watching football and hanging out. I actually stopped everything I was doing and just took it all in. My home filled with memories, treasures and keepsakes, my family and the general ambiance that is my life. I found myself sighing and smiling all at the same time. I realized how content and happy that I am. Which after the past 34 years is more of a triumph then I realized until just now. To say that the past couple of years have been 'trying' would be an understatement, at 34 years old I feel like I have the soul of someone who has lived twice that. It has taken a lot to get to this moment. A lot of tears, loss, struggles and fight. I appreciate those small moments in time when everything is peaceful and more importantly content. I try day by day to trust in these moments, to accept that maybe from now on, this is what will be. But I find that it is hard. When your life has been turmoil for a long time, a sudden reprieve is really hard to trust in. These small moments in time when I can hear my husband yelling at the refs on TV and the laughter of my son at how excited his dad is getting, when I can look around and think of happy memories associated with the belongings we have acquired over the years. I sigh.

The road to this moment has really never been smooth. More of a dirt backroad, bumpy, rocky, with cliffs on one side and trees on the other. Lots of forks in the road, twists and turns and mountains. With an occasional stretch of smoothness, that usually leads to a series of switchbacks. The Road of Life. I really wish looking back; I could have had a road map. If only it worked out that way. Of course thinking now, there really isn't anything that I would change, because it made me who I am today, brought me to where I am today and has taught more about myself, others and life, than a smooth road would never have done. I can appreciate what I have right this moment; I feel it in my soul, because I know what being without this feels like.

There are essentials to a happy life, something to do, something to love, something to hope for, and something to believe in. Happiness and sadness tend to run parallel to each other. When one takes a rest, the other one tends to take up the slack. But to even come close to being happy you have got to do one thing. You have to make peace with yourself and where you came from. You have to come to terms with everything that has happened to get you to this moment, every tear, every triumph, and every trial. You have to consciously work on it. Ignoring it, "forgetting it," and burying it, never ever work. Because it is always there, just waiting for that weak moment to come forward again. It takes strength and courage. You have to want it.

The little things ARE the big things in life. A night at home with my family, the laughter of my son, the armchair coaching from my hubby, the coziness and warmth. These little things are what make me happy and content.

Frederick Koenig said it best when he said....
"We tend to forget that happiness doesn't come as a result of getting something we don't have, but rather of recognizing and appreciating what we do have."

It is also appreciating all that I have done to get here.

Life's Ambiance.

Unconditionally-With Conditions

You really can't love unconditionally. People can burn and beat love out of you. They really can kill it, and it's not your fault you don't feel it anymore, and how liberating it is to finally realize that. Love isn't for better or worse, through thick or thin. It damn well shouldn't be.
Dr. Kay Scarpetta, Red Mist. By: Patricia Cornwell

Everyone is always searching for that elusive unconditional love. The older I get the more I realize that it is a myth. The premise that unconditional love is impossible will have some people shaking their heads at me, I know. But if you stop and think about it, how can you love another person without conditions? Why would you really even want to? It is the ultimate sacrifice of you. To give someone that much control really is to say, go ahead hurt me, lie to me, abuse me, use me and I will still love you. Ummm, no. Well not in my world anyway. I love my husband with every ounce of my being. I love his good points, his strength, his integrity, his dedication and I love his flaws...the ever procastinating, the channel flipping, the hours he works. I love all of him. I don't try to change him, mold him or want him to be anything other than who and what he is. I love him unconditionally-with conditions. I love the man he is and the man he wants to be. Unless that man one day decides to hurt me, then its game over. People never walk into a relationship and settle down expecting the worse to happen, ok well most of us don't. But as the adage goes, Shit Happens. If one day he were to morph into Captain Asshole, then those conditions would come into play.

Love should mean, love me for me, flaws and all. Don't try to change me into someone else, trust in me, challenge me, and allow me to grow. Love my independence and my spontaniety. It should mean that you can count on me to always be faithful, always love you for who you are, to always challenge you and be excited to watch you grow. I will unconditionally love you for you, unless you change for the worse, and then well, there are conditions. Man or woman doesn't matter; we all should enter into relationships with established conditions, and love unconditionally only as long as those conditions are being met. Why would you sacrifice yourself, allow your self to be abused, because you unconditionally love your partner, husband, wife, and lover? There is no honor in selling yourself short.

For better or worse, through thick and through thin, in this day in age are being taken totally too literal. Granted every relationship has its ups and downs in the normal course of life and that is fine, you weather those and become a stronger couple. Life happens and stress occurs. But if these stresses lead to your wife cheating on you, or your boyfriend taking all his aggrevations out on you, physically or mentally, then why would you continue on with this person? You can't love without conditions in a marriage or relationship because to do so is like selling your soul.

I asked on my Facebook page once, what people thought about unconditional love. Their answers surprised me, not going to lie. They for the most part said it doesn't exist. Unless it was the love of a parent to a child, and even then that doesn't happen all the time. But that is a whole 'nother blog. I loved one woman's response the best, she said; "The only unconditional love that existed, was the love of a dog." I think she may be on to something there. I do have to say that there is one form on unconditional love that I do believe in, and that is to love yourself. You may beat yourself up, get angry at yourself over mistakes, but you have to always love yourself. That isn't the easiest thing to do, I know, believe me I know.

Always love unconditionally-with conditions. For the simple reason, you are worth the sun, the moon and the stars. No one should ever have the power to hurt you.

Done With Toxic People

Never be bullied into silence. Never allow yourself to be made a victim.
Accept no one's definition of your life; define yourself.
~Harvey Fierstein

The only person in this world that you have 100% control over is yourself. How you react to life, to people, to upsets and happiness is completely dependent on you. Granted, your reactions to things that life hurls at you is typically based on your experiences, your past, your inner strengths and weaknesses; however, sometimes in life you need to delve past the typical and reach a part of you that remains unexplored.

We all have scars, some visible, most not. You cannot go through life without getting them. Once they are healed, they are your battle wounds. They symbolize some life lesson, some part of your life that hurt you, but you fought back. Once that scar has healed, it is a reminder that even when you aren't feeling particularly strong or feel like fighting, you have before and you can again. To go through life without getting scarred at some point, is not to have lived. How can you truly appreciate the good, without having triumphed over the bad?

There are times in life when silence is called for, taking the high road and not allowing yourself to be pulled into someone's drama, until it comes to the point of you feeling like a victim. Never allow yourself to become victim to another's drama, another's toxic behavior. Their issues are only your issues if you allow it. Speak up, do not allow yourself to be bullied into silence in order to keep the "peace" or avoid causing ripples. By doing so you place yourself into the victim role and that is no place to live. Never allow yourself to become the victim, take control of yourself, your reactions, and define the role that you want to take.

Over the course of our lives, we will be faced with toxic people. It's inevitable. It sometimes is easy to allow them in, allow their poison to affect us, at times it seems impossible to get away from them. The hard ones are the ones we are related to, married to, work for. It is in these relationships that the cycle of unhappiness, fear and often self loathing continues round and round like a merry go round you can't get off. Round and round you go, never realizing that there is so much more out there. That you deserve people who respect you and love you. Toxic people are incapable of seeing anything or anyone but themselves. They build themselves up by tearing you down. Some feel trapped, their self confidence eroded over the years, their self esteem so damaged that they have no idea what it is like to feel like they can take on the world. They become the victim of their very own life. By allowing another control over you, how you think, feel or view the world, you are denying the very thing this world needs most - you.

Found My Inner Bitch

I have found my inner bitch and ran with her.

Bitch. Yeah I said it, or rather, wrote it. I am not ashamed of it either. As is quoted above, I have found my inner bitch, not that hard really, she isn't quiet for long. I refuse to quiet her, stick her in some corner of my soul and tell her to behave. Nope. She is the side of me that is the strongest, the smartest and the one in complete control of herself. She values her judgement, makes her place in this world, and will never back down from anything. She stands tall, takes life by the balls and says, we have done it your way, now we do it mine. She is outspoken, intelligent and never allows herself to get pushed around. She stands tall and will hold anyone's gaze, because she can, because she is who she is and she doesn't care what anyone thinks about her.

We all have an inner bitch. We have just been taught that it's not "lady like" to let her out. That by playing the passive, demure, quiet woman is what is expected. Well, I have never really been quiet, sure as hell never been demure and passive, aww hell no. But it takes its toll, seriously. People like to try and make me feel bad, that standing up for what I believe in, going after what I want or taking a stand about something, is a bad thing. They call me a troublemaker; try to put me in my "place." Thing is, everyone in my life knows where I stand, that I am always there when they need me, and if something is wrong, I can be a force of nature. And I am so ok with that.

Do you have a moment in your life that you look back on and wish that you had stood your ground, stood up for yourself when no one else would? Sure, we all do, me included. Do you ask yourself, why you didn't? Why did you not trust your own voice, your own strength, you own place in this world? Why did you silence your inner bitch? Consequences, the subsequent fall out of standing firm, of putting someone in their place? This I understand, but I also understand that if something is worth fighting for, that it is all worth it. I know the first time for a lot of women is the hardest. We want people to like us, often times at the expense of ourselves. But it doesn't have to be like that. I don't care if people like me, but they have to respect me. I know that some people in this world for not good reason other then because they can, will not like me. I am ok with that; chances are I wouldn't like them either. But this does not give them the right to disrespect me. Same goes for you, you must command respect, demand respect.

You can not control how the world sees you, you can however, control how you react to it. Never fear your own voice, because sometimes in life that voice is the only one that will stand up for you. Never allow anyone to belittle, demean, torment or put you in your place. You all have it in you. I know it can be scary at first; you will take some heat and be temped to run or shut her down again. But it will get easier, like the saying goes, practice makes perfect. I am always around for pointers too.

Being a bitch isn't a bad thing. Being a bitch means you have decided to become totally in control of yourself and your life. It means that you are no longer a pushover, no longer a doormat, no longer that sweet controllable woman. The woman who allows herself to be used, lied to and put down, no longer exists. Command respect, stand up for yourself, because it is time.

It is time to release your inner bitch.

True Reflections

I will not be known in this life for my body.
(Well except for my boobs-they are pretty popular.)
What I will be known for is my mind, my writing and the
lives that I touch. The outside is just window dressing.

Lately I have been spending time with this group of women. Ranging in age from 27 to 50 (*something*). Each one of these women comes to this group from a completely different walk of life, background and location. Each one is spectacular in her own way. There are teachers, writers, horse trainers, stay - at - home moms, dentists and more. These women over the past months have become my sounding board, my encouragement and my constant source of humor, ohh hell they make me laugh. They are supportive, generous, and simply amazing women. It is probably the most improbable group of women to come together. But it works. Each one of them has a story and lessons they can teach the others, they are so open, it's refreshing. Each one brings something different to the table. And I love them for it.

Last week the subject of wanting to lose weight came up. One of these ladies, made a comment that she was going to use us to help her lose weight and stop eating badly. She planned to announce her weight and we were to talk her out of bad eating choices. Actually not a bad idea, kinda of the angel on one shoulder and the devil on the other side. We would be the angels, *as I type that I laugh as we are all so far from angels*. But what happened after she came forward with this, kinda of stopped me in my tracks. Every one of the women came forward with something about their appearance they wanted to change, fix, lose, tighten, etc. Not one said I'm ok with me. Now I know we all have things about ourselves we want to change, and getting healthier is an awesome goal. But is not one person happy with herself as is? These women are beautiful, successful, loving and funny. However each one came forward to announce her flaws. I admit-I did too. Though not at first, at first I just observed. The thought occurred to me, instead of being our own best friend, somewhere along the lines we had become our own worst enemies. Me included, hell if anyone outside of myself said the things I say in my mind, I would bitchslap them into next week. I accept no disrespect. But yet, I disrespect myself on a daily basis, by wishing I were thinner, prettier, better some how. It seems to be a common belief that one must be thin to have value. That the numbers on a scale determines one's worth. That when someone is not a size 2, that he or she is worthless. Not only from society's point of view, but our own. We seek some level of perfection that is set by others. We step on scales, look in mirrors and degrade ourselves.

I know in this lifetime, I will never, ever be known for my body, *(well except my boobs, they are pretty popular)*. What I will be known for is my mind, hopefully my writing, and the lives that I touch. I will be known for who I am - the real me. The outside is just window dressing.

Next time you are standing in front of a mirror, look deep into your eyes, for it is in your eyes that you will see your- true reflection.

Rock Bottom

*Rock Bottom is good solid ground, and a dead end street
is just a place to turn around*

Rock Bottom.

To me, Rock Bottom was a starting point. Solid ground on which to begin to build the foundation of my life. If you are lucky, that foundation is built when you are a child. But if you are like me, the foundation of my childhood had so many cracks in it, I needed to rebuild it. When one bottoms out in life, it is not the end of the world. Though at the time, it sure as hell feels like it. But there is truth in the saying that the only way you have to go from the very bottom is up. You have to want it, though; you have to want to start rebuilding a solid foundation first, in which to place the rest of your life on. That foundation is your soul. You must make it solid and strong and plant it firmly on the ground. But its construction is completely up to you, where you build it, how you build it and how fast. All hitting Rock Bottom is, is giving you solid ground on which to build.

I spent a few hours talking with a girl who had hit Rock Bottom, she wanted to die. She was tired of the constant struggle, the finding her place in this world, to wanting to feel peace. She was hundreds of miles away from me, someone I have never met, yet I felt her struggle as if she were in the room with me. Knowing that as hard as I tried, as much as I could give, the only one who could lay the first brick of a new foundation on which to build her life - was her. I could be there, I could lend my shoulder, my ear and my heart, but I couldn't do it for her. What I tried to show her was that she mattered. All day I have thought about it. Rock bottom hurts like hell when you hit it, you are disoriented, ashamed, sad and scared. You look around and see nothing. You panic and you fret and you often just want to lay your head down and say, no more. I am tired. But it is in these moments, the darkest ones of your life, that a spark is born. You plant you feet and get your bearings. You get fired up and you fight. You fight for yourself.

Your life may be upside down, but all that is doing is giving you a new perspective. A fresh new start, fresh new chapter. You control it completely. You grab life by the balls and say, now we do it my way.

And then you do. One brick at a time, you lay your new foundation and you build. Slow, steady and the way you want it. You learn to value yourself and what you contribute to your world. You do what you have to do, to first survive, then get strong and then happy. Proud of the fact that even at your worst, you never totally gave up on yourself.

Even when it feels like the world has given up, that the bottom is speeding up at you. Just remember what I told you, Rock Bottom is good solid ground. A solid start to what will become your life, as you make it.

Kick some ass ♥

Not Under My Heart, But In It

Not of my flesh and blood, nor bone of my bone, but you are still miraculously my own. I have never forgotten for a single minute, that while you didn't grow under my heart, you grew in it.

I always said from the time I was old enough to have such thoughts, that I was never going to get married, never have children, never going to settle down. I was going to travel the world, move to Boston and write. I was going to live my life through characters in books and through articles for the Boston Globe. I would have occasional boyfriends, but no one was ever going to get my heart. Seriously though, from as early as I can remember, this was my dream. People at arm's length and never close enough to hurt me. Vulnerable was not a word in my life's dictionary. Until that Spring in 2004, when I met the man I was to call husband and his son. My heart never stood a chance. All the best laid plans, all the walls that I had so artfully constructed, fell apart. Almost in an instance, though I fought it for awhile. Who were these two people that wanted to invade my life, my very solitary life? I was 26 and very comfortable on my own. Independent, strong and definitely not looking.

Once I finally stopped fighting it, and began what would be my life from then on, meeting the guy's son for the first time should have been awkward at least. But nope, not even for a second. From the moment he and I first laid eyes on each other, and had our "sword" fight, him with his crutches (he had broken his leg) and me with a plastic sword from the fair we were at, we were immediate best of friends. Our bond was instantaneous, and would only grow stronger. He was 5, I was 26. I was well on my way to jaded, coffee drinker writer who spent time in coffee houses and at my desk creating lives for my characters.

Instead because of them, I became a character, in my own life. I never thought I would ever be a wife, let alone a mother. To say I was a bit lost would be an understatement. But a year later, the man proposed and four months after that, we married. The during the ceremony I presented the kid with a family medallion, a small silver pendant with three interlocking circles, representing that I was not only marrying his father, but him too. That we were a family, a strong family. And that while I would never be his "mother," I swore that he would always be my son. That while he may not have grown under my heart, he grew in it. Our bond is that of a mother and a son, except, we are friends first. We talk about everything and anything, we plan for the future, we laugh, we have fun. We became a family.

Needless to say that while our lives meshed seamlessly, it wasn't the case with his mother. I have made it clear from the beginning, that I never wanted to replace her, be her or take over. That the kid and I were the best of friends first and foremost. That while I have come to feel him my son I know I am not his mother. Her jealously at the beginning was expected, and I rolled with it. Thinking that over time it would lessen and she would see it for what it was. It hasn't, actually has gotten worse over the years, but I refuse to ever let it shadow what he and I have. This kid is so special, so intuitive, so creative, so mischievous, and has best damn giggle. I will not allow her negativity into our relationship. Never have I spoken negative to him about her, she is his mother and I respect that. But seriously the shit she has pulled over the years I think to ultimately try and drive me away, has made me shake my head. My wish is that someday she will just get over it and understand. Of course knowing now what I didn't know then probably will never happen. She really isn't a nice person, actually not really at all. She lives in a world of make believe and her selfishness continues to surprise me.

However, because of the love I have for the kid, I will take it from her. He deserves all the love and things that this life has to offer. The Man and I intend for him to have it. Love, strength, boundaries and knowledge. A solid base for the kid to build upon and become a man. He turned 14 recently, and while he may have his teenager moments already, he will never lose that charm, that devilish grin and eyes that will make your heart melt. He is truly a magical kid and I am so fortunate that The Man and The Kid decided to invade my life.

Looking back now, this morning, I can't imagine my life turning out any other way. I have to say that I am excited to see the man that my stepson will grow to be. His heart and his innate want to help others are tremendous. He sees the world very similar to me, as a chance to reach out to people less fortunate or sad or in need. Just as not long ago, he pulled together some of his toys because he wanted to give them to some children that had lost all of theirs. Or how excited he gets to volunteer with me for The Buddy Walk for Down Syndrome, and how his teachers say that he always stands up for the special kids at school, befriends them and treats them as he treats everyone, without judgement. I am proud to call him son, though not of my flesh and bone, but of my heart. ♥

Own It, Own You

Have faith in your dreams and someday, your rainbow will come shining through. No matter how your heart is grieving, if you keep on believing, the dream that you wish will come true.
~ Cinderella

The older I get the more I realize through all the dark times that can happen they are never permanent. They will eventually fade, and it is up to me to determine what is left behind after it's over. It would be so easy to just shut down and coast... but that is no way to live. Got to keep believing in something. The best thing is always to believe in you.

I wonder sometimes why this is so hard. Why believing in oneself at times is almost impossible. Why are we our own worst enemy? If we can't believe in ourselves, have faith in our abilities, understand our strengths, then how can we expect anyone else to? Why is it that we feel the need to have the world validate us? The only opinion in this world that we really need to be concerned about, is our own. When we are sad, grieving, lost, it is not the world's responsibility to find us, fix us or heal us. It is totally on us. When did we lose faith in ourselves? I hear people say all the time, "when I am stronger" or "when I am happy" or "when I finish grieving", then I will live again. They shut down and coast through life; they make a life while never actually living it. They place their dreams, hopes and desires in a box and put it in the closet. Coasting becomes habit, habit becomes character and character becomes their life.

I am guilty of this, myself. Tired of life blows as I call them, I just stopped at some point. I put my dreams and belief of myself in a box and called it good. I was too bruised, too jaded, too tired. This worked for me for awhile, until it just didn't work for me any more. I started my writing again, started believing in myself and taking my life back. Life can throw me body blow after body blow, and I will take it head on, deal with it and then move on.

Nothing will knock you down forever, only thing that keeps you there is yourself. You are responsible. While you can not control others, their actions, their issues or their lives, you can totally control your RE-actions to it. What are your dreams? What do you want for you, RIGHT NOW? Write it down, make a to do list. A **To Do for YOU List**. Then start crossing things off, baby steps at first, but the more you believe in yourself, the better you will do. As Cinderella says: *"Have faith in your dreams and someday, your rainbow will come shining through."*

Stop waiting for the world to validate you, you validate yourself

Leave the Pieces Where They Fall

I was never one to patiently pick up broken fragments and glue them together again and tell myself that the mended whole was good as new. What is broken is broken - and I'd rather remember it as it was at its best than mend it and see the broken places as long as I lived.
~Margaret Mitchell

For almost everyone, there are moments in your past that are shattered. By mistake, by circumstance, by your own hand or the hand of another. Moments in our collected history that if given the choice, we would forget about. But our memories are long and instead of leaving the pieces as they fell, broken, we often find the need to fix them. Like a valuable glass vase that has shattered, there are moments and memories, spans of time from which we have come, that for some reason, we think with enough tears and glue we can somehow put it back together again and make it whole. What we fail to see is that, what has happened to us in the past are the moments that led us exactly where we are today. Cause and effect, will always be a driving factor within our lives. We can relive the past over and over and over again, make the same mistakes repeatedly, but what we will never be able to do, is fix it. It is over. You can not go back and undo what has already been done. You can't go back and be a different person, make someone different or change anything that has happened. Why would you want to? Everyone has something in their history that hurts, that makes them sad or angry, even fearful. But the thing is - it *is* over. You can't take your past and glue the pieces back together and think it good as new. Because not only will you only be able to see the brokenness of it, but it will never be as strong as it was when it was at its best. You can't change what has happened, what you can do is learn from it, make peace with it, and then move on.

I know that it is hard to accept. If only things had been different, if only I had this life growing up, if only if only if only. Thing is, the "if onlys" of our lives are meaningless. They didn't happen, you didn't grow up in some idyllic setting, with Ward and June Cleaver as parents, it happens. It shapes you, it scars you and if you let it, it will overwhelm you. The past can be like an evil merry go round if you let it, round and round you go, over and over and over, and if you never get off, you never move on, all you will be able to do, is go in circles. You can't fix something that was broken, you can't mend it and and glue it and have it as good as new, because it won't be. There will always be the scars from when it was broken. Eventually the glue will fail and it will all fall apart again. Better to leave it broken, see it for what it was and then work on making something better, something stronger. Make your future as you want it, shape it and then live it. Leave the past behind you, the lessons you learned take with you, but leave the ghosts and the hurt where it belongs. It has no place in your future.

Accept everything there is about you, I mean everything. The beginning of your story, every chapter you have added since. Make peace with yourself. Make peace with what has happened in your life, in your past. Then leave it there. Someone once said, *"I never told you life would be easy, I just told you it would be worth it."* Use that one foot you have planted in your past, to propel you to your future. Leave the broken pieces where they fell, take sometime to appreciate everything you have gone through, conquered and withstood, fell pride that you have gotten this fair and know that it doesn't end here.

Take back control of your life. No excuses, no *"if onlys,"* your past is not who you are, it is simply what got you here to this moment today. You got it from here, make it brilliant.

Forgiveness

How does one know if she has forgiven? You tend to feel sorrow over the circumstance instead of rage; you tend to feel sorry for the person rather than angry with her. You tend to have nothing left to say about it at all.
~Clarissa Pinkola Estes

A couple days ago, I was having a conversation with friends about forgiveness. About when it was the right time, right place, right frame of mind to offer it and actually mean it. At what point, do we forgive someone? Of course each instance where forgiveness is wanted or needed is different, the level of wrong, the extent of the transgression against us, determine our frame of mine when contemplating it. I have always thought that some things in life are completely unforgivable, still do actually. But I have started to wonder, if in not forgiving and moving on, is not for the person who hurt us, wronged us, but ultimately, for ourselves. That by holding onto that anger, hurt and sadness, are we sealing off a critical part of ourselves that really needs to be healed? In forgiving someone, are we giving them the power to hurt us again, or are we giving ourselves the power to move on?

As I have journeyed through life, I have been hurt, and I have been wrong, just like you and everyone else in this world. I share this part of my journey only for perspective, on October 31, 2011, my mother committed suicide. Alone in a motel room, she decided that she no longer wanted to be a part of this life. At the time of her death, we were estranged. Had been for about a year. My life with her had been a struggle from the time I was a child until the day she died. Undiagnosed bipolar disorder, had robbed me of a mother I had so desperately wanted. What I got instead was a woman, who never admitted she was ill, who never saw the damage her illness created. She would build me up, only to tear me down. The lies and manipulations that plagued my childhood, I carry with me today. As a child I worshiped her, I believed everything she told me. I believed her when she made claims against others, against family members. I fought battles for her; I cried for her; I begged for her love. I sold my soul, my very being, to be the best daughter that I could be. Over and over again. It took me 32 years to understand that I would never be able to. I was in my 20s, when I realized that my entire life to that point, had circled around her. Her wants, her needs, her manipulations and lies. I had lost a huge chunk of my life, my self and my confidence. It is a hard reality to face when you realize that your mother is incapable of love. Her love, her attention came with a price and for years I had paid it. Until the time came, when I could no longer. I had shouldered the responsibility of her illness, her highs and her lows for too long. No one else but my sister saw it, no one understood. Outsiders thought we were the worst daughters in the world. She had told them that, and they believed. There came a breaking point and it was in that moment when I realized I could sacrifice myself no longer. I let go, and I walked away. I carried with me, the hurt, the anger, the feelings of failure and defeat. I had tried and I had failed. I could not be the daughter that saved her mother from an illness that had controlled her for her entire life. You cannot help those who do not want it. I harbored resentment and anger for the entire year we were apart. I needed to heal. I had a strong hope, that in losing me, she would see that she needed to face this, that she would find the strength inside of her, begin to understand her worth and fight a battle that only she could fight. I had hoped and dreamed that she would become the mother I had always wanted. Bipolar robbed her of that which was her. It took from her the very core of her being and replace it with something that was completely opposite of who and what she truly was capable of being. Because her bipolar went untreated for so long, she spent many years looking in the mirror and seeing a person she did not recognize or understand. Not only did bipolar rob her of her sanity, but it robbed her of the ability to see beyond the space it dictated her to look. She could no longer tell reality from fantasy, and she walked in a world no longer her own. And as time went on, she pulled it around her like a blanket. Never did she take responsibility for her own life, her own well being. In death, as in life, both my sister and I shouldered the blame.

Jeanette Walls said once *"When people kill themselves, they think they're ending the pain, but all they're doing is passing it on to those they leave behind."* With my mother's death came, anger and sadness, shock and emptiness. And ever since, I have tried to put the pieces in some semblance of order. But what I have come to the conclusion, that there are some things in life that will never make sense. Some parts of life that the only thing you can do is make peace with. Forgiveness means letting go of the past. It means letting go of the hurt and the anger and moving on. When you forgive, you in no way change the past - what you can do is, change the future.

I want to get to that point when I think about her, with what she did and how life was with her. I want desperately to think of the happy times that there were, and to release the anger and the sadness. I know it has no place in the future. I think I finally get that in forgiving her, I can release the power of the memories that hurt, that fill me with anger and sadness. I am releasing it and saying - no more.

Not yet. Forgiveness, real honest forgiveness, doesn't happen over night. I find that with each day, with each thought of her, the anger has lessened a little, but the sadness, not so much. I will know when I am there, as you will. Forgiveness is not only anyone's schedule but your own. It is in your own time, on your own terms. But I am really starting to believe, that is something that eventually needs to happen. I will never forget, but there will come a point when I forgive.

For her, for myself and for the future.

Coming to forgiveness is not for the one that hurt you, it does not invalidate your hurt, what it does, is say that you no longer will allow the actions of another to hurt you, that you release all the pain and the anguish, because it is time. Because holding on to it, never gives you the space is needed to heal.

Line in the Sand

At some point, you have to make a decision. Boundaries don't keep other
people out. They fence you in. Life is messy. That's how we're made. So,
you can waste your lives drawing lines. Or you can live your life
crossing them. But there are some lines...
that are way too dangerous to cross.
~Meredith Grey

When we set boundaries in our lives, we set limits not on others, though
that's what we tell ourselves, but on ourselves. We draw a line in the
sand and say, do not cross. We do not allow people in for fear that they
will hurt us. We have all been burned so many times, that these
boundaries are more of a protective shield than anything else. But it is
only in our mind. How many of you have people who simply disrespect
the boundaries you have in place, who do as they wish, when they wish
and be damned with the consequences? Do you fight with them, throw
accusations and demand they respect them? Do you hang your head and
wallow in the unfairness of it. Do you draw that line in the sand and dare
them to cross one more time? Which they do, always. Life is messy, it is
unpredictable and uncharted and every day is something new. Because if
it isn't, well then you aren't really living. Maybe you have so effectively
fenced yourself in that you forgot how to get out?

Don't get me wrong here, certain boundaries are important. Knowing
what you will and will not allow in your life is sacred. Standing by them
even more so. Not allowing people to cross the sacred ones and to stand
up for yourself, is highly critical. However, what is also critical is
making sure that those same boundaries, do not fence you in from your
own life. What is also wicked important is making sure the boundaries
that are set in your life are yours. Never operate within boundaries that
someone else has set for you. You alone are responsible; you are your
own person. I don't care if it's your family, your spouse or significant
other. Only you can set your boundaries, as only you can stand up for
them.

Boundaries. Walls. Fences. Fortresses. To some extent we all have them.
We tend to try and keep our lives as organized, logical and contained.
We worry about others will do, we try to control situations and we build
our walls higher when it doesn't work. Effectively walling ourselves in

as we are trying to keep the world out.   Boundaries more often than not work against us. I am not talking major, this is my line and if you cross it, the consequences will be dire. I mean the boundaries where we try and control everything and everyone, that when something does not go our way, we retreat and react. I mean when something upsets us, makes us angry or sad and we react with everything we have inside to make it stop. Instead of stopping and for once realizing that we can not control, manipulate everything in life. That WE need to cross our own boundaries sometimes and realize that life is messy, sometimes is hurts and sometimes it fires us up but it is up to us how we handle and react to it that matters.

We are not made to live in tiny little bubbles. Life is going to happen regardless of what you think you can and cannot control. Why waste your time drawing lines in the sand, when you could be doing something so much more worthwhile? Like being happy. Like finding work you love and doing it. Like being confident and strong and realizing that you have the power over your own life and then do something with it. We all need to stop walling ourselves in and walling life out. People are always going to things that upset us; we are always going to come across situations that break our hearts. Building stronger and stronger walls are never going to protect us from that. Life and all its ups and downs will continue to happen, the good the bad and the ugly. That is what makes it so amazing. We all need to stop standing by a line that we drew in the sand and we need to cross it. We need to stop worrying about everything we can't control and worry about the things we can.

Don't live your life standing safely behind your walls. Go out and make mistakes, make a mess, make a fuss, make a noise, but most of all make the most of your life.

Life Isn't Always Sunshine and Rainbows

Every one of my scars both inside and out, tell my stories. Of how though wounded, I fought, I conquered and I eventually healed. My scars make up who I am, who I was and remind me of how life can deal some nasty blows, but eventually I will heal.

Life isn't always sunshine, rainbows, puppies and smiles. Actually more often than not, it can be downright dirty, unjust and unfair. Life can deal blow after blow and isn't always satisfied with just knocking one down, it needs to kick you a few times to drive its point home.

One tries not to take it personally, shit happens after all, but there are times when it seems to keep slapping you in the face saying, nope, no happy for you today, or tomorrow or maybe even next week. You look around you and wonder, what did I do, to bring this upon myself?

When your life is in turmoil, you have to wonder, why? Doctors call with bad news, your children are failing, your wife is unfaithful, you are out of work and bills are stacking up. You tell yourself that it can't possibly get any worse and your car dies on the way home. You fight with your best friend, your family is attacking you for reasons you will never be able to fathom. You want to crawl into a corner and wave a white flag at life saying, seriously- enough already.

You get so tired that all you want to do is hide, because what is the point of putting yourself out there, when apparently you have a giant kick me sign on your back that everyone can see. Sound familiar? You wake up in the morning and instead of being optimistic, the day in and day out of reality has you wanting to pull the covers over your head. You have had it, no more. Why bother?

Reality makes for a cold bed fellow though, your thoughts will swarm around inside your brain, as you search for some internal off switch. You get up anyway, because really, what else do you do? You dress and you have your coffee and you go about your day. Eyes cast to the ground because you do not want anyone to see the defeat in your eyes, the sag in your shoulders, your ever fleeting will to live slowly fading. But you go, you get up, you put one foot in front of the other and you brace yourself for what the day will bring.

Day in and day out it is the same thing. Little grievances add up, til one day you look in the mirror and say, screw it. You lose your temper, your emotions fire up and you get your fight back. You look yourself in the eyes and say enough. Cause see, your reality is what you shape. You have to have the balls to make the changes you so desperately need. You have to stand up for yourself, even if you are standing alone.

Rid the people in your life who have no place in your future, shed the negativity and realize, that life can deal you blow after blow, but you can fight back. You get knocked down again and again, you get back up. Cause that one time you don't, the one time you accept defeat and not pull yourself together is the time it would have worked.

Above all in life you must be true to yourself, if there is something in your life you cannot put your heart and your soul into, and then take yourself out of it completely. Accept everything about yourself, I mean everything. You are you and that is the beginning and the end- no apologies and no regrets. Life may knock you down; it may bloody your nose and break your heart. But those pieces can be picked up, and slowly put back together, again and again til you get it right. Bernice Reagon had it right when she said "Life's challenges are not supposed to paralyze you, they're supposed to help you discover who you are."

Who you are, who you can be, who you will be is not defined in the moments when you are on top, it is defined in the moments that you are at your lowest point. When you are one step away from throwing in the towel, but don't. When the walls are closing in and you are faced with uncertainty, with fear and filled with exhaustion, you become paralyzed for a moment and then you discover your strength.

The journey of your life each day begins with a single step.

What Goes Around Comes Around

There is a destiny that makes us brothers: none goes his way alone,
All that we send into the lives of others comes back into our own.
~Edwin Markham

Have you ever heard of the Threefold Law or Law of Return? Basically it states that whatever energy a person puts out into the world, be it positive or negative, will be returned to that person three times. "Mind the Threefold Law ye should, three times bad and three times good."

Meaning if you go out into the world and practice random acts of kindness, offer respect to others and treat people the way you wish to be treated, then with the Law of Return, it will circle back to you, three times more powerful. Kind of, what goes around comes around.

However the flip side of that is if what you put out into the world is anger, negativity and hate, then that is what will return to you three times over. One of the things that as I get older I realize more and more, is that as long as I live up to standards that I have set for my life – be honest, be hardworking, treat everyone with respect and kindness - then I can sleep at night knowing that I gave my best everyday. Don't get me wrong though, not everyday is sunshine and rainbows, obviously there are days when I want to pull my hair out, scream unladylike words, and put people that are making me cranky into a headlock. Days like these make anyone cranky, but it is how you react and handle them that show your true colors. I may do the unladylike words like a champ, but I deal with whatever is going on to my limit. I never allow anyone to push me past that line. Self control is something I value immensely in my life. If someone disrespects me, I will call them out on it, or not, depends on the situation, but I will not let their disrespect or ignorance push me past the point where I drop to their level.

Let Karma deal with all the people in your life who aren't worthy of your attention. Why worry about what they say or do? Let them carry on and make complete fools of themselves, while you live life to standards you set. Do what you will and harm none. Why give anyone a second thought who doesn't deserve it? Work hard, be honest, stand up for what is right, do for others, smile at strangers and live the life you want. As long as you can sleep at night, then that is what matters. Giving someone the power to rile you up over something that really in the scheme of things, doesn't matter, is simply a waste of energy. Remember how people treat you is their Karma, how you react is yours. Their negativity, their disrespect and their lies will return to them threefold, your honesty and kindness is what will come back to you.

Your actions are your only true belongings. You cannot escape the consequences of your actions. Your actions are the ground upon which you stand. Edith Wharton said it well, *"People pay for what they do, and still more, for what they have allowed themselves to become. And they pay for it simply: by the lives they lead."*

Remember what you send out to the lives of others, will return to your own.

Just Like That

How would you feel if you had no fear?
Feel like that.

How would you behave toward other people if you
realized their powerlessness to hurt you?
Behave like that.

How would your react to so-called misfortune
if you saw its inability to bother you?
React like that.

How would you think toward yourself
If you knew you were really all right?
Think like that.
~Vernon Howard

Feel, Behave, React and Think. These four actions we do every day, normally without thinking. We fear the unknown, we allow people control over our emotions, we take even the slightest blip in our day to heart and overreact, we get home after a long day of running, working, taking care of everything it seems and then we look into the mirror and see ourselves. We second guess decisions made our thoughts, choices and then we swear that we will do better tomorrow. We will conquer, we will be fearless, we will let stuff roll off our shoulders and we will fall asleep content with what we accomplished.

Then we wake up, and none of that actually happens, sounded good in theory but in a practical world yeah didn't happen. A cycle is born and the fear, the powerlessness permeate everything. We feel inadequate in the face of a challenge, we fall apart if something bad happens, and then we blame ourselves. That's life right, to be expected? **Hell NO!**

The more you identify and face your fears, the less power they hold over you. You got to face them. Then start your day, without any fears. Why worry about something that hasn't happened yet? Give no one power over you, period. I don't care who they are, the only person with power over anything you say, do or feel, is yourself. No one has the ability to hurt you, unless you give it to them. And why would you do that? Take your power back. Behave like that, own yourself. Stand up for yourself, and never give anyone your power. One of my favorite sayings is, Shit Happens. It does, and there is nothing you or I can do to stop it, prevent it or send it to someone else. You are going to hit bumps and glitches in life, some big some small, but hell, deep breathe, and roll with it. Do what you gotta do, take care of it. Cry if you need to; scream if you have to *(my favorite)*. Hold yourself together, take care of it and realize that a glitch in your life, doesn't define it. Shit happens, you deal with it, and then you move on. How would you think about yourself, if you knew you were all right? Here is my stunning revelation, you are. You are perfectly all right. You are who you need to be, who you were meant to be. If you want something different, then work towards it, you will still be alright. You want to make changes, great! You will still be all right while you are making them. Think like that.

You are your thoughts. Your thoughts are your life. Make them random, make them strong, make them powerful and make them with the faith in yourself. You are definitely, all right.

Breathe. Believe. Receive.
Then kick some ass.

The Academy Award goes to-the Narcissist!!!

Are a woman's lies merely an indication of her own twisted reality or does she consciously know she's lying when she sets out to make herself look the perfect, innocent and injured party?
~Tigress Luv

Reality.

A simple word, but one that for some, is so hard to face. Instead some will twist it, color it and shape it to fit into only what they can handle. What fits into the lies they have told the world, their family and most of all themselves. They manipulate situations, lie and the sad part - not really for them, but the people are around them - is that they believe it. Honestly though I wonder, do they even realize that they are lying to themselves? Or is their perceptions of reality so distorted, so colored by the lies that they have told, do they actually believe it to be true?

I refuse to play a starring in role in someone's fantasy world. If someone feels the need to try and control me, my life and the lives of people I care about, I have no time for them. You all know what I am talking about here and have probably had one or two in your life who you have been faced with - the Narcissist. That one person that will twist reality to suit their needs, making everyone but them, look like the bad guys. Who will play the victim role like an award - winning actress just to get the attention they crave.

Their desperate need for control, shaping everything they do, say, and ultimately believe, is like a veil over their eyes. They feel the need to bring people down, in order to validate their very existence. They are manipulators and control freaks, with no thought to anyone but themselves. They are incapable of love, of any real feelings. But rather are more in love with the impression they leave on others. These types of people are falsely in love with only those who believe in these false impressions; will only tolerate you as long as; you play along with their fantasy, with their lies. When one sees through their facade, sees through the twists and turns of their lies, to the true self behind the mask they wear to the world, the Narcissist will often become outraged, full of disrespect, disdain and contemptuous dislike for the one that dared look beyond what they wanted you to see.

In essence, the Narcissist has mastered the power of words, without understanding the power of substance. While they talk and they talk, their words, when probed, mean nothing. Just because you say the same thing twelve different ways, in a variety of flowery descriptions, does not make it reality.

For example there is this Narcissist I have the pleasure of dealing with personally, she will tell you that she is the most open and honest woman who walked the face of the earth. When in reality is she manipulative, pathological and lacks the emotional substance of a basic human being. This woman hates me, loathes me, I know this, everyone knows this. But yet in a communication she states how appreciative she is of me, how she respects me. Honestly I almost spit coffee out when I read that one line, as she has been nothing but disrespectful, with her lies and interference in things in which she has no place. But this Narcissist makes it a point to make it her place; she takes control freak to a new level. As long as people play along with her delusions, the false impressions she presents to the world, and then she will pretend to be sweet and loving, key word there being pretend. Nothing in a Narcissist's world is based in fact, in reality. They will say the right words, but never be able to back them up.

The sad thing is, the Narcissist believe her lies. I can't imagine a world where I would need to lie to myself in order to function. With me, what you see is what you get. I can back up my words and I do so by the life that I lead. I have follow through on my promises and hold a firm grasp upon reality. I imagine that it is a lonely existence waiting for people to see through the image to what lies inside, knowing full well that they will see the truth eventually and will walk away. When one bases a relationship - be it friends, lovers or family - on lies and manipulations, the truth will eventually come to light and the Narcissist will be alone.

Draw the curtain, the fraud is over. May you all be immune to the deceptive words of your own Narcissists and may you have the joy of calling them out whenever you get the chance.

The Weight of the World

*I would shrug my shoulders, but the weight of the world rests there
and I am afraid it would cause a catastrophe.*

Do you ever feel like you are carrying the weight of the world on your
shoulders and that one wrong move will tip the balancing act and all
come crashing down. Do you sometimes wish you could set the weight
down and rest a bit or let someone else carry it for awhile? But you
continue on, in hopes that with each step, the load will lessen a bit. In
reality though, it never really seems to lessen. In fact more and more
seems to get added to it, until you are not sure if you can even stand, let
alone walk with it any more. But somehow you do, you find the strength
you need, from some part of you that even you didn't know existed until
you needed it. It amazes me the strength that one can find even when so
exhausted, so stressed that it seems impossible to continue on. But you
do, really what other option is there? Give up? Not in my world.

Sometimes in life, we get bogged down, we get tired. So many things
seem to come at once and we have to shoulder it. Shoulder it, work
through it and try not to collapse. Sometimes it is hard to see an end in
sight, so heavy the load. At some point enough has to be enough, right?
There has to be a stretch of time where everything magically goes right,
everything fits into place and the world revolves without us having to do
anything, but be.

As I sit here writing this, in a few stolen moments in my day, I sigh. Just
the thought of a stretch of time, with no stress, no drama, nothing to
handle, deal with or get through, makes me smile. Well smile and shake
my head knowing a day dream when I see it. Or maybe not. Maybe there
is a way, to once in a while, set the load down, catch your breathe and
just be. There has to be a way to get life to leave you alone for awhile, to
decompress, to put your own head and thoughts in order. There has to,
because how else can you help everyone else, if you can't help yourself?
If you are so drained, so emotionally exhausted, so stressed, how are you
supposed to keep putting that aside, day after day to handle everything
for everyone else? You do, months on end, even years until that one day
that suddenly arrives when you just can't shoulder that load any more.
You have to put it down for awhile, or else it will crush you. It is not
weakness; it is the epitome of true strength.

We all have to realize we are human. We may climb the mountains, we may move them out of our way, we may play the hero, but we are human. We cannot be expected to handle everything all of the time without some break. We have to learn, teach ourselves, to set the load down once and awhile and focus on ourselves. We have got to hold a hand up and say stop. Stop the drama, stop the stress, stop going around in circles about problems that really just never get solved and move on. Life is too short. If we don't look up once in awhile we will miss it, we will miss it while we are fixing everything and anything, but ourselves.

I wish for you strength to continue on, and the knowledge that while it is hard now, over time you will lose that weight on your shoulders and be free.

Just remember, you are strong enough, smart enough, and tough enough. Know that setting that load down for awhile, to catch your breath, is not weakness. It is a sign that you value yourself enough to rest for awhile. It is a sign of true strength. The world will not shift off its axis, the sky will not come falling down, I promise. It will be there to pick back up when you are ready, but only when you are ready.

One foot in front of the other, one day at a time. Pieces will eventually fall into place and your hard work; your perseverance will pay off. You will be free and you will be ready to take on the world.

Deep breath, you got this.

Toughen Up-
This is Reality We Live In

The thing about life is that you must survive. Life is going to be difficult, and dreadful things will happen. What you do is move along, get on with it, and be tough. Not in the sense of being mean to others, but being tough with yourself and making a deadly effort not to be defeated.
~Katharine Hepburn

Regardless of whatever you are facing in your life right now, regardless of how hard, how desperate, how awful it may feel, you have to face it. You have to deal with it, head on, and not give it any more space in your world. You have to make changes, you have to face your demons, you have to stop avoiding, you have to see things as they really are, and then do something about it.

Over and over lately I keep hearing people say, *"I'm not strong enough"* or *"If I just ignore it, it will go away"* or *"I am scared to be alone."* Or the one that makes me cringe the most *"I give up."* It makes me crazy when an otherwise intelligent person, decides that they are not worth fighting for and just accepts whatever life throws at them. They will go to bat for everyone else but themselves. Seriously people, the only person in the world that will ever stand up for you; go to bat for you, is YOU! If you sell yourself out, you don't plant your feet and square your shoulders and say Bring it on!! And handle your business, who will? Own your life, your world and realize that you are worth fighting for.

Growing up with a bi-polar mother, this was hard for me to grasp when I was younger. It was easier to take the blame, shoulder all responsibility for anything and everything that had gone on, real or imagined. I would go to bat for everyone else, stand up and fight for every underdog I could find. But what I would never do is fight for myself. I was tough all right, hard as nails on the outside. But I absorbed every body blow that life threw at me; I took it and allowed it to happen, because it was easier. Easier. Yeah, easier for everyone else. Not so much for me. Took me a long time to realize that. Honestly what I realized lately, is that I stand up for me when it's not family or people I care about. How weird and backassward is that? If some guy is rude to me out in public, or some random person tries to take advantage of me, I handle them. Right in their place they go. However, if its family, then I take it and take it. Never do I correct their misconceptions, or tell them they are wrong.

Well, I do now - most of the time. I am still working on it. But for the longest time, I thought surviving was walking away from all the bad. But then I realized that sometimes in simply walking away and not handling it, didn't stop anything. That you have to speak up for yourself, you have to toughen up and do what is right for yourself. You have to stop giving up on the one person in this world that should never give up on you, yourself.

So what if your heart is broken, so what if you are afraid, so what if you fear changes... Hearts heal, courage is found and when you face what you fear the most, you adapt. You toughen yourself up and you handle what needs to be handled. There is no giving up, there is no, "I'm not strong enough" there is no ignoring it or taking it because that's easier. Sometimes you have to make a mess, you have to shake things up and sometimes you just have to grab life by the balls and say, I am worth more, I am strong and I will get to where I need to be, because I want to and I will make it happen. Feel that strength start in your belly, feel it grow and learn to trust yourself.

What you don't do is quit, ever. You survive, you dig deeper than you ever have before, you will find every ounce of strength and courage you will ever need, not in some book, or in anyone else, and you will find it within yourself. You do what you have to do, and you do it for yourself. Take that pride and take that sense of accomplishment and use it to build a new foundation on, use your strength, your heart and your survival and make the changes, fight your battles and never, ever give up. Life will come along and deal you some nasty blows from time to time; it will knock you down and hold you there if you let it. It's ok to take some time to get your bearings, catch your breath, but then, come out swinging.

Never accept defeat. Never accept things can't change and never ever accept that this is the way life should be. Be the force in your own world and handle your business. You all have it in you, you just have to dig a little and find your tough.

Life is a Balancing Act

Don't get so busy making a living that you forget to make a life.
~ Dolly Parton

You wake up in the morning; you get out of bed, begrudgingly most days. You shower, grab some coffee and head out to work. Day in and day out, same routine. It is comfortable and completely uneventful. You find for awhile, you like that. Get up, go to work, come home, watch tv, go to sleep and get up and do it all over again. Days blend to weeks, weeks to months and on to years. All of a sudden one day you look back and wonder where all the time has gone. What have you really accomplished? What have you done worth mentioning? What fun did you have, lives did you touch, things did you do?

By focusing all of your time and attention on work, did you forget your life? "I gave at the office" doesn't mean your whole world. Focusing all of our efforts on our responsibilities and not on the things that make this life worth living is a completely backwards way of living. If all of your energy is being spent at work, all of your being and efforts going into a job, where does that leave your life?

Each one of us has infinite value, and each one of us has the ability to make a profound difference in the lives of our family and friends, simply by being there, being a part of their worlds. Just by being who we are, we impact those around us. By the nature of our lives, our humor, our love and by the example we set. Not by how busy we are, how important we are, or how important and demanding our jobs are. Our example, our value to the ones in our lives, is us. Getting caught up in a rut of work all day and expending minimal effort to anything else, is not the path to happiness. Focusing one's whole life and time on responsibilities, without taking time for what is truly important in life, abandons all hope of happiness and fulfillment. When I die, I want my tombstone to read, "Inspired others" rather than, "Never missed a day at the office."

Work is important, I get that. But what it shouldn't be is all encompassing. It should not be the reason you wake up in the morning and why you go to bed at night. It is not your identity. It should not dictate your life and those lives of the ones you love all of the time. It is a necessary part of life, but it is not your life. Getting so caught up in the day to day, busy making a life, you forget, to actually live that life. You stay so busy working, it is comfortable and controllable, and there are procedures in place for everything. Not like life, where there are no guarantees, no playbook. In life you have to wing it sometimes and while that can be scary at times, it is also thrilling.

Life is what you make it, always has been, always will be. If you were to stop right here and honestly look at your life, what would you see? If you see things that you want to change, then by all means, change them. You have the power to do with your life whatever you want. It is just making that effort to follow through. Stop talking, start doing. Stop being an observer in your life and be a participant. This life is the only one we get, make it count.

Would You, Like You?

Self-respect cannot be hunted. It cannot be purchased. It is never for sale. It cannot be fabricated out of public relations. It comes to us when we are alone, in quiet moments, in quiet places, when we suddenly realize that, knowing the good, we have done it; knowing the beautiful, we have served it; knowing the truth we have spoken it.
~Whitney Griswold

Do you like yourself? Honestly. A simple question really, but one that so many have a hard time answering. Honestly answering. Usually it's a quick, well of course, followed by a just as quick disclaimer. If I were this, had this, did that, then I would. Leading one to hear more self doubt, than self respect. I asked some readers awhile back a simple question and the answers were all over the place. I asked, *"If you were to meet yourself on the street, would you like you?"* Some said no, probably not. Some said at first, then they would probably annoy themselves and others replied with a resounding Yes! I would.

I am not sure what my initial reaction would be honestly if I was to meet myself for the first time, but I have a feeling that I would like me. I would like me enough to get want to know myself better and even maybe be friends with myself. After of course picking apart my own flaws, I am human after all. What I do know without question is that I would respect me.

If there is something about me that I don't particularly like, I change it. Simple as that. If I do not like a side of myself that being around certain people bring out, I stop hanging around those people. If I am constantly reacting to a situation that I have some control over, I try to take steps to fix it. I have enough self knowledge to know what I am ok with and what I am not ok with, and I have no problem voicing this to someone who disrespects it. Whether or not it continues is up to them, whether or not I allow it, is completely up to me. If at the end of the day in one of those quiet moments I can look back on what I did, what I said, positions I took and battles I may have fought, and know that I did it in accordance with my belief systems, my conscience and followed my heart to do what was right, what was just and what was good, then I count it as a good day. If I looked back and see situations that I could have handled better, could have walked away from and didn't - and I am not proud of myself in those moments - I make mental note to do better, see what I could have done differently and then move on from it. Mentally beating yourself up is useless, making mental notes on how to do better is fantastic.

You can not buy self respect, you can not discover self respect, you CREATE self respect. It is entirely up to you. If you don't like something, change it. Yes it can be hard, yes it can be a battle and yes you may have to hurt someone's feelings. But if it means being able to look yourself in the eye, to become stronger and stand up for yourself, than do it. Never allow anyone to shadow your self respect. Value yourself more than that. Be someone you would want to hang out with, laugh with and cherish. Take those negative thoughts you have, examine them, learn from them, and move on from them. Look at the people in your life, examine them, learn from them and see if they deserve a place in your future. Respect yourself to know what you need, do not look to anyone else for that.

L.M Montgomery said it best in her novel "Anne of Green Gables":
"Isn't it nice to think that tomorrow is a new day with no mistakes in it yet?"

Start your tomorrow clean and make it one that you can look back on, and realize that, knowing the good, we have done it; knowing the beautiful, we have served it; knowing the truth we have spoken it.

Well Done Is Better Than Well Said

Remember, people will judge you by your actions, not your intentions.
You may have a heart of gold - but so does a hard-boiled egg.
~Author Unknown

I have spent more time lately paying less attention to what people say and watching more of what they do. The phrase *"Actions speak louder than words"* coming from a writer may seem a little off, but my action is in my writing, so I am covered, *(well at least in my mind)*. But it is a phrase that I have been thinking about a lot lately.

People talk a lot, act very little. They speak of what they want to do, see, experience, but never seem to actually take a single step in the direction of making it reality. It seems sometimes the more they repeat the words, over and over again, the more they actually feel like they have accomplished the actual act. Somebody who says over and over again that they wish they had more time to relax and kick back, never seem to find it, people who want to go out and do good, help someone less fortunate, never get beyond the initial thought. People spend more time dreaming about things, than actually doing them or taking steps to make them happen. Quite frankly, it is a sad reality.

I mean, I know that we can't do everything at once, but we can do something. Words become meaningless after constant repetition and no follow through. It is like telling your daughter that you will find the time to take her to a movie or out for "just you" time, and never following through on it. In actuality, words without action are broken promises. Broken promises to yourself, to your family, to anyone who believes in you. If you are constantly saying one thing over and over and doing the complete opposite, after a while your words become empty. After a while, the people who look to you will stop, they will stop believing. Life is to short for empty words, you must feel the power of the words to motivate yourself to actual DO the words.

Words are powerful, statements are powerful. Ironically, making a statement with words is the least effective method. Making a statement, than following through with action, be it taking the time for someone who loves you, pursuing the dream you have had over and over, taking that first step and building the path from your words to your destination, that is powerful. That has meaning. You don't have to do everything all at once, but you have to do, something. Anything to prove that your words are not empty, that you are not just saying them to say them. That you actual believe in them as well. Your actions show the power to your words, as much as your inaction does.

Maya Angelou once said, *"I've learned that people will forget what you said, people will forget what you did, but people will never forget how you made them feel."* You make people feel by the things that you do, the lengths that you will go, not only for yourself, but for others. It doesn't even have to be some grandiose thing; it's the little things that matter in the day to day of our lives.

The older I get the less I listen to people's words and more I look to their actions. If someone is constantly saying one thing and doing another, or not following through on anything, I tend to spend less and less time on them. Life is to short and I want people in my life that mean what they say and say what they mean, then do it. Not just say pretty words that lack any substance because there is no action behind them.

We often will have to remind ourselves, we are worth more than empty words. And we will learn to see the same in ourselves. Our actions and reactions define who we are and where we are going.You are either moving forward or standing still, and while standing still at times is ok, if it is a constant pose, repetitive in itself, then I think its time we all stop and re-examine ourselves, then do something to make it right.

Dancing Skeletons

If you cannot get rid of the family skeleton,
you may as well make it dance.
~George Bernard Shaw

Every family had a closet somewhere filled with skeletons, right? Those things that everyone knows, but no one talks about. Past mistakes, bad choices, lies that had been told in a moment and then carried on throughout the years. Each skeleton representing something someone doesn't want to come out.

Years can go by and one never thinks about them, brief memories may flash inside their minds and they shudder thinking about what would happen should one of the skeletons get loose. Life goes on, it spins away from that point in time when a decision was made to hide a truth, and before one knows it, that lie or bad decision has become the very foundation of which the family has been built upon.

Over the years, skeletons may get added to that closet, things families just don't talk about, things that no one wants to see the light of day. Things that could damage or destroy the very fabric of a family. If no one talks about it, it never happened. Normally it is something so far in the past, the children of the family know nothing about it, the elders forget and life goes on. But there is something to these skeletons, something in the closet that makes them very restless. As the old saying goes, the truth has a habit of coming out, usually when you least expect it.

What gets to me is the ripple effect of one of these skeletons. One lie begets another and then another is needed to cover the first two, and now after a few years, the skeleton gets buried further back in the closet and new ones are piled on top. Until that point in the future when the restlessness gets to the skeleton, or someone slips or discovers something, and all the family can do it watch that damn skeleton come dancing right out of the closet. Because it is what happens in that moment, that defines the future of the family. Some will continue to tell stories, some will anger, and some will feel ashamed. Some can have the foundations of their lives crack and destroyed as they realize that everything they ever held true was in fact, not even close. Where do you go from there?

When I was 21, my mother informed me that the man I thought was my father was in fact, not. At the time, she claimed she had no idea who my father was, and that was all she would say on the matter. It was kind of a "Hey, here's what I did, and now you know and nope, don't want to talk about it any more". As much as I tried to get my feet back underneath me, I was rocked. Who wouldn't be, right? All of a sudden a skeleton that had nothing to do with me, and everything to do with her, had now become my skeleton to deal with.

She felt resolved, she felt better, so I inherited it. Lovely. It took more than 10 years for her to give me any further information, but finally, she gave me a name. Took me about 15 minutes on the Internet and I found him, pictures of him and frankly there was no doubt, he was my father. The resemblance was amazing. He also lived 20 minutes away from me, for my entire life. Needless to say, I reached out, we made contact and holy hell, guess what, not only did I now have the answers I needed, I also all of of a sudden had five brothers and sisters. Talk about a skeleton, this one came out, dancing, singing and in my face.

Thing is though, I am not a fan of skeletons. I am not a fan of the little white lies people tell each other. Families should be based on truth, the good, the bad and the ugly. That is what makes family. If at any point in time something occurred that one does not feel sheds the most flattering light upon them, then take control of the situation at the time it happens and do something about it - right then. Don't wait 30 years for something to come out and let those most affected by the mistake pick up the pieces.

I have met a couple of my father's kids. I met a sister yesterday and I have to say that it was pretty amazing. To meet a complete stranger who oddly enough, is so much like you that it's scary. It is definitely a new adventure and nice to know that every once and a while, something good can come from one of these dancing skeletons.

Stop the Ride-
I Wanna Get Off

*Being in control of your life and having realistic expectations about your
day-to-day challenges are the keys to stress management, which is
perhaps the most important ingredient to living a happy,
healthy and rewarding life.*
~Marilu Henner

Stress management. Some days I would like to find the person, who
coined this phrase, sit them down and explain "Life" to them. That is
Life with a capital "L". I know that I am supposed to manage stress, that
I am not SUPPOSED to let stress manage me, but I live in reality and
sometimes, reality is really just too much. There are days, where if I bite
my tongue any harder, I am apt to bite it off. Days when the filter
between my brain and my mouth is on the verge of disintegrating and I
may just speak out loud, the words I have been holding back, or fighting
back, which is usually the case. Days that are spent handling and doing
and making decisions and facing problems and issues that all seem to
happen at the same damn time, regardless if I want them or not.

Sound familiar?

Like right now I have a bunch of little annoyances that need attention,
little on their own but when put together, a big mess. There is a list of
things a mile long that I need to do, a couple of major things that I need
to face and take care of and, oh by the way, there is an unknown arsonist
in my neighborhood apparently hell bent on burning houses down.
Lovely. I live in Maine, in the woods. Away from the city, away from
crime. Yet I just had a knock at my door, it was a fireman telling me to
be vigilant. Stress Management doesn't have a play in the book for
adding this to the mix. Ever feel like holding your hands up and yelling
"Stop the Ride...I Wanna Get OFF!!"

Ever have one of those days where you keep looking to the sky to see if
it is a full moon? When you look around you and wonder, is it you or
has the whole world gone crazy? Even the most laid back, take - life- as -
it - comes people, have days like this. I love the quote *"I try to take life
one day at a time, but they all seem to attack at once."* Sometimes, life

can get so overwhelming, so stressful, that you really don't even know where to start. You feel so completely boxed in, your muscles clench, your blood pressure goes up and it takes the simplest thing to push you right to the edge. So what do you do or not do? A lot of people I know, just shut down and refuse to deal with it, some drink, some exercise, some yell into pillow and shake their fist at the sky. While a temporary relief maybe, doesn't really solve anything. So how do you manage your stress?

A few tricks I have learned: Don't sweat the small stuff. Pick your battles wisely. Not everything is worth fighting for. Take deep breaths. Count to 10. Think before you speak. Walk away. Make a list. Set YOUR priorities. Stay true to yourself. Breathe. One thing at a time. Trust yourself and your instincts. Ask for help. *(I am so not good at this, but I try)*. If it's a problem that you have had for years, just be done with it. Face it, deal with it, and move on. Don't let fear hold you back, face what needs to be faced, find your voice, and handle it. Know that it's ok to set the stress down for awhile, take a break, get your strength back, and then handle your business.

Remind yourself this: many of the great achievements of the world were accomplished by the tired and discouraged who kept on. Live. Love. Dream. Make it happen. Don't give up.

Tell My Fairy Godmother....
She's Fired!

It is my belief that we all have the need to feel special. It is this need
that can bring out the best in us, yet the worst in us.
~Janet Jackson

I was having coffee with a friend the other day; our coffee talk is pretty amazing. It runs the gamut from kids, to work, to gossip, to deep and personal. From shared experiences, life, stress, to what we are going to cook for dinner. Mainly, we talk about life and the craziness of it. We talk about being exhausted and how hard it is to juggle all of our responsibilities, to be what people expect us to be, handle everything and then some, all while attempting to keep a smile on our faces. More like, forget the smile; I would be happy with not having bags under my eyes on a daily basis.

The other day it was one of those conversations were all we did was bitch about everything we had to do, keep track of, handle, juggle, decide on and make time for. Our stolen time for coffee was a break in reality that for a little more than an hour we both cherished. We get each other, she understands what it is like to try and be 15 different people in the course of a day and how that after awhile, it gets so old, you just want to throw your hands up and say, *"The hell with it, I quit."* Only you can't quit, because you don't have the time for it.

After she left, I ran some errands and all the while I was thinking. It appears that more often than not, we all spend so much time taking care of everyone else, from work, to family, social commitments, kids, school, sports etc. that we probably by the end of the day, forget that we are actually first and foremost, a person too. We cook, we clean, we pay bills, we plan play dates and outings, manage schedules, parties and carpooling. We work full time, which are more roles that we play, more things to handle and deadlines to meet and bosses to make happy. By the time we get home and plan dinner and actually cook it, we want to fall sleep at the table. But things need to be done and it appears that 9 times out of 10 it is up to us to make sure they get done.

Have you ever noticed how no one seems to notice exactly how much you do in the course of a day? Well, they don't notice until you stop doing it, and then it is like the world comes crashing to a halt. Do you ever wish your damn Fairy Godmother would show up and wave a wand and make you a queen for the day? Hell, forget a whole day, even for a couple of hours. A span of time where it's all about you? I mean you, as in who you really are, not you wearing one of the many hats you don every day, not the you who takes care of everything and everyone, but just simply, you. Do you even remember who that person is? Don't you wish that someone would take the load you carry, set it down and take care of you? Sigh, I can just imagine you reading this right now and shaking your head and saying, *"Yeah right, as if."* More often than not, it comes down to you, to treat yourself. And, if that is the case we all know where on your list that is, right at the bottom. Who has the energy? How many of you just wish, someone else would make you feel special, do something just for you, not for anyone else but you? It is not being selfish, it is being human.

I would worry more about it, but I am too tired. I think I need to find that Fairy Godmother of mine and tell her she is fired. Maybe I can find a new one at WalMart, one that grocery shops or something. Yeah I know - fairy tales don't actually ever come true. But a girl can dream, can't she?

True Strength Is Asking For Help

Happiness can be found, even in the darkest of times,
if one only remembers to turn on the light.
~Steven Klove

Have you ever sat alone with yourself, lost in your thoughts, feeling completely and utterly, alone? Feeling like no one in the world will understand what you are going through, what you have gone through, what you are facing? Do you feel the darkness creep in, fogging your brain, and making you want to lie down and sleep forever? Do you find that you wish someone would reach out and take this burden from your shoulders, as you are just to weary to carry it any longer? Do you sit in a group of friends and feel like no one understands your pain, your grief, your sadness? How could they understand everything you have been through, how could anyone?

You walk through crowds, surrounded by strangers, and feel like you are apart from all of them. That their lives and their happiness are somehow unobtainable for you. You feel envy and jealous when you glance into the lives of others - you want what they have. Do you ever stop and realize, that just maybe, they are looking at you and thinking the same thing?

One out of every 10 Americans suffers from clinical depression. Depression can be triggered by any number of factors in one's life: chronic illness, death of a loved one, abuse, divorce, job loss - the list goes on. The big thing to remember with this is that you are not alone. You are not alone in your suffering, in your history, in your sadness. Though it feels like it, feels like there is this huge gulf between you and the people you love. You don't want to talk to your family, your friends, for fear that they will never understand, never see it, will blame you and tell you to just get over it. You would, in a heartbeat, but you find that you can't. Your world becomes so shrouded in the gray that even the sun seems to have lost its shine. You retreat further and further into yourself, you withdraw. Friends and family see it, see you retreating but say nothing. Depression has become, *"the elephant in the room."* Out of fear, out of weakness, out of lack of understanding, the elephant or issue remains where it is, and all that refuse to talk about it or see it for what it is, gingerly tiptoe around it. You feel even more cut off from the world. How can anyone understand what you are feeling when you really don't understand it yourself? You decide to let it go, you don't reach out for help, you don't call your doctor, your therapist, your family. You leave that elephant in the corner of the room and hope one day it disappears, but it never does. As the days and weeks wear on, you get tired, more tired than you ever thought imaginable. You just want it to end, you want to sleep forever. You think of how much better the world would be without you, no one would even notice. You just want the pain to be over, you want happiness, but you just know somehow that it's not for you to have.

It is in the darkest moment that one must turn on the light. Cast the shadows back into the corners of your mind, and find a way out. You have to want to get better, to feel happiness; you have to fight for it. And know that you are not alone in your fight, there are so many out there who face the same battle as you. A strong person is one who asks for help when they need it. There is no shame in asking for help, no shame in talking about what you are experiencing and the struggle you have been in. The only shame to be had, is NOT asking for help. You may not see it now, but you are so important to people who love you and to strangers you have yet to meet. You are worth fighting for, always. Remember that, hold it close to you, and repeat it over and over, you are worth fighting for. Your life, your presence matter and you are not alone.

Reach out. Ask for help and fight. If you find yourself completely lost, and you feel like there is no where to turn, call this helpline,
1-800-273-8255(TALK).

Just never give up and remember that sometimes in tragedy, you find your life's purpose.

The eye sheds a tear in order to find its focus.

Crossroads

Sometimes life doesn't give you a choice. Sometimes it takes all control from your hands and says, "Hang On - Ready or not."
You either roll with it or you break that, is your only choice.

Sometimes in life, you have no control. Gasp! Really? Forces outside of yourself, bigger than you, collide and take the reins and leave you standing there. Breathless. Confused. Lost. Bewildered is a good word. Walking along your road of life, you come around a bend and - BAM! A crossroad. Not one that you had planned on, walked towards or even knew was there. You stop, confused. You look around and suddenly realization dawns. You have no idea how you got here, have no idea which road you will be forced to take and you have absolutely no control or say in which direction you will go. You have relinquished control without meaning to, wanting to or even knowing. Allowed only a glimpse of each path before you, you have no idea where they lead, how long they go and who you will need along the way. Darkness surrounds you, fog swirls in and you feel completely in the dark. Scared. Turning around and going back is never an option. Not going forward isn't either. You will have to face what is in front of you, one way or the other. Denial isn't your nature and not even a possibility. What is going to come will come. The only choice in the matter that you have left is how you will handle it.

One goes through stages when faced with a situation that you have no control over. Fear. Denial. Anger. Sadness. Finally, acceptance. If you are like me, accepting a loss of control over a situation that directly impacts my life is beyond difficult. I react, I handle, I take care of. I move mountains if I must. I face things and stare them down. I am strong; I am in control of my own life. Right? Well yeah, sure. But only until I am not. When life decides a curve ball in is order, I am in whether or I want in or not. It is coming up to my crossroad and knowing that I am either going to get the road on the left or the road on the right. I know which one I want. I also know I have zero say in the matter.

I have a few days before I find out which road will be mine. I will use these days to learn some more about myself. I will prepare for both roads. I will go inside myself and I will handle what I can. I will try different perspectives and I will firm up my strength. I will play the hand that I am dealt, and I will win. Because, while I have no control over which road I will be given, I have complete control over how I begin. I know that I will face whatever comes with my usual strength and determination. I will walk either road with humor and with love. I will handle it. Because that is the only option really. Handle it. Face it. Deal with it. Play the hand you are dealt and play it well. Who cares if it is a shitty hand? It is your hand. How you play it will determine how you take a situation that is out of your control and live it. You may not want to; you may be scared and feel very isolated. But you play it. Folding is not an option. You find your strength, you square your shoulders and you handle it.

When you come upon a crossroad in life that is not of your choosing, that is completely out of your control, accept it. Use your fear to propel you forward and your strength to see you through. You can handle everything and anything life throws at you. You never lose control of that. Your reactions and your determination will see you through. Never doubt that for a minute. You may not be able to control that life gives you, but you will always be in control of how you face it, handle it and get through it.

I Want a Pause Button, Damn It!

Have you ever wished that life came with a pause button?

Have you ever felt some times in your life that the world must be spinning a little bit faster or time has somehow sped up? That things in life were going a little too fast, were too much and all at the same time? A period in life where you just couldn't seem to catch your breath? It seems lately, my *"To Do"* list keeps growing, my calendar keeps filling up, and if one more crisis arises I may start wearing a cape and pretending I am Super Jenn. So many places to get to, things to accomplish, cleaning to do and work and laundry and...and...and - I'm tired. I was driving home from work today and running through everything I have to get to, get done and remember this week. From work stuff to home stuff, to appointments, games and commitments. Honestly it made me even more tired just thinking about it. It also does not leave me much brain power or energy for my writing, my Facebook page and myself. Don't get me wrong, I love my life. I love my job, my family and my friends. I just wish that life came with a pause button. I don't want a rewind button; sure as hell do not need a fast forward button - just simply a pause button. A simple button that will stop the spinning, the running, and the constant doing, long enough for me to catch my breath.

Even as I sit here in a stolen moment and write this, I have to really stop my thoughts and focus. I can think of no less than a dozen things that need doing. But they can wait, or at least that is what I am telling that little voice inside my head. For right now, for this moment, I am stealing Jenn time. The dishes can wait, as can the vacuuming and the bills. I do not have to be any where for a few minutes. I am creating my own pause button. Sitting on my deck, at home in the woods and I am content. I feel like I may have pulled one over on the clock and the "To Do" list and it feels pretty amazing.

When I got home, I sat for a few minutes. I shut off my brain and simply listened to the wind in the trees, the birds chirping and some angry turkeys somewhere. When those voices started to creep in saying, *"you should be"*, *"have to be"* and *"get going already"*, I silenced them. It was in this quiet stolen moment when I had an epiphany. I can only do so much in one day, in one hour. There is no crime in stolen moments to catch my breath. It is the same for you. We have to learn to create our own pause buttons. To put aside the stresses of everyday life, the chores and just simply; be. It is far too easy to keep running and running til you drop from exhaustion. Or make ourselves sick because we are trying to be everywhere at the same time. We can only do what we can do. We can move mountains with our will, balance babies on one hip and make dinner at the same time. We can care for our families; work full time jobs and handle everything. Of this I have no doubt. If we can do all of this and more, than we sure as hell can make our own pause button. We have to. Call it stolen moments, call it me time, call it whatever you want, but make it happen.

Life is what it is. You can either go through life at mach 10, constantly doing, and miss things. Or you can learn to create your own pause button. Stop. Catch your breath. Focus on you and than, carry on.

I am off now to simply be for a few more moments. I have a date with reality soon and I hate to keep it waiting.

Stepping Stones

I do not ask to walk smooth paths nor bear an easy load.
I pray for strength and fortitude to climb the rock strewn road.
Give me such courage and I can scale the hardest peaks alone,
And transform every stumbling block into a stepping stone.
~Gale Brook Burket

"Do not wish for an easier life; wish instead to be a stronger person." I love and hate this quote at the same time. Why would I not - while making my way through life's rock strewn roads - wish for an easier life? It would make me human after all, wouldn't it? Who wants struggles and challenges day in and day out? Who wants constant stress, worry and exhaustion? Life may be what we make of it, but when situations and problems arise, completely out of your control, what are you supposed to do? Walk away? I have been tempted over the years, but I am not that girl. I turn, square my shoulders and say, *"bring it on."* In all seriousness though, when I said; bring it on, I didn't mean - and on and on and on...

I asked my Regulars on my Facebook page, *"In what way are you better off today than you were five years ago?"* The answers honestly left me speechless and very contemplative. Such strong life moves by women leaving abusive relationships, quitting drinking, adopting and having children. I was proud that these people were a part of my world, inspirations all of them. I thought over my past 5 years, quite frankly just the fact that I have made it through them is what I am most proud of. I know myself better, have a bit different perspective on a lot of things and yet feel more scarred by them, then healed. Probably a bit more jaded if that is even possible, definitely more tired and yet optimistic at the same time. Each stumbling block has turned into a stepping stone, it had to. Otherwise I would still be face planted on the ground wondering what the hell was going to knock me down next.

Life is what we make of it. Our past and current struggles, problems and stumbling blocks are really only a part of it. A large part at times granted, but just a part after all. Everything we have faced, continue to face, are strengths that we are acquiring through it all. Battle scars and life knowledge give us confidence in ourselves that we can handle anything life decides to throw at us, even when we are exhausted and beat up. We have to continue on, because we only get this one life. We cannot allow our fears; our moments of weakness determine our fate. We have to find that courage that got us to this point and rely on that to get us to the next. We never know what is right around the corner for us and yet we need to make that corner, because just around it, good or bad; is our life. Even though you are tired and scared, you have to make that turn, pulling strength and fortitude from inside yourself. Its ok to admit fear, just do not be controlled by it. Life is scary. The unknown is scary. New beginnings, new chapters in your life, fresh obstacles in your path will be handled. Because you can, because you are strong enough and because it is in you to see everything life gives to you through.

Never stop wishing for an easier life, but never stop praying for strength, courage and fortitude either. No one said life was supposed to be easy, they just said it would be worth it. Take your triumphs and moments of happiness and hold them close. Use them as catalysts to get you through the dark moments. Always remember, they are but moments, use them as stepping stones to the next chapter of your life.

Never Settle

He felt now that he was not simply close to her, but that he did not know where he ended and she began.
~Leo Tolstoy

Normally I am not a sappy type of woman. I despise romance novels, the Twilight saga and anything that remotely smacks of the cutesy, gooey or overly sentimental. I am not into chick flicks, and for the most part avoid anything too "girly" for lack of a better word. For the longest time, I avoided everything that had anything to do with love. I had reality, and in reality, what I saw was what I got. I was ok with that. There were no feelings, not wanting and no chance I was going to get hurt. I had walls 12- feet thick with steel re-bar in the middle and no door. OK, maybe not literally, but my defenses were solid. Until they weren't, not when this man came waltzing through them, like they were air and he was in my life, like I wanted him there. Which I didn't. Not at first.

A friend of mine asked me last week, what is true love? I bit back the sarcastic reply that was quick on my lips, and actually thought about it. I looked at that guy who had waltzed into my life and never left. It's been eight years and we haven't missed a beat. I looked at him and saw; well I saw a whole lot. I saw my past and my future, my beginning and my end. I saw two halves and one complete whole. I saw happy and sad, strength and weakness and I saw, love. Real love. It is knowing without knowing. It is that fit, the melding of souls that can't be seen only felt. It is the feeling of a part of your soul becoming whole as it seamlessly fits with another. It is not work, there is no effort. It simply happens on a karmic level. It is the feeling of coming home, of finding some part of yourself that you didn't even realize was missing until you find it. There is no question, there is no doubt. True real love simply… "Is" You hear it in a sigh, you see it in a gaze, and you sense it while in its presence. Like air, it just simply is. It is the feeling of being whole.

Real love isn't work. There is no thought process that goes into it. It is either there or it isn't. You can't force it, hide it or deny it. If you walk away from it, you will leave that piece of you behind. You don't find it, it finds you. Once you experience it, you never really question it because it just is. I look at my husband now and sometimes it is hard to tell where I end and he begins. We are two distinctly different people who form a whole that is as solid as the ground I walk upon. I don't doubt it; I am not scared of it. What I am is in awe of it.

Never settle for less than you deserve. Not to sound trite here, but the quote, *"Life's not the breaths you take, but the moments that take your breath away"* is about perfect. Relationships require work, love not so much. If you have to work at making someone love you, than it's probably not the real thing. It should be effortless and smooth.

Never, ever settle for less than you deserve or for less than that perfect moment, that will last a lifetime and take your breath away. ♥

The Hypocrite's Life

*The true hypocrite is the one, who ceases to perceive
her deception, the one who lies with sincerity.*
~Andre Gide

Hypocrites. You all know at least one. The person who shows one personality, one face to the world, yet behind closed doors is a completely different human being. Who acts all Polly Anna in public, but in truth is so far from that public persona it is ridiculous. The coworker who acts all industrious when the bosses are around then gives you their work to finish when they are gone. The mother who claims to have her children's best interest at heart and is so involved in their lives, when in truth she is too busy taking care of herself that she really just can't be bothered. The storybook family whom all envy when they meet them, who hide more skeletons behind the walls of their home then you could imagine. At least with criminals, you see the bad they have done, but with hypocrites, they lie and they manipulate, losing all sense of whatever integrity they may have had at some point. So important to them, public appearance, public perception, that they will do or say anything to get you to believe them. It drives me crazy.

People who manipulate, people who lie, people who pretend to be someone they are not, are on my very short list of people to avoid. I have no place in my life for them. I don't care about anything other than the type of person you are. I could care less about how much money you have, what you drive, who you know. It is all about who you are as a person, for real. Not the phony front that they put up to appear to be something they are not. I have been around long enough, to see right through it. What gets to me is the damage they do. It is one thing to lie to yourself if you can't face a certain truth about yourself, but to take that and morph yourself into something you are not, to the point that they actually believe it, just to look *"good"* in the public eye? Nah, just doesn't make sense to me. I like when people are the *"what you see is what you get"* type. This is me, the good - the bad - the ugly. I know I am not perfect, but I also know that you can go into any facet of my life and it will not change. I am who I am. I know I can be outspoken, at times judgmental and really sarcastic, but I am also, giving and loving and good person. People in my life know where I stand at all times. But that is me. I do not need to lie to myself or to the world in order to get people to like me. Not like some people in this world and it really drives me crazy. Can you tell?

I say the words: *"This is your life. Own It!"* all the time. I really mean it too, own it. If you are open and loving and a good person, then *be* that person. If you are selfish and only concerned about what you want, how you feel and not about anybody else, then fine, be that person all the time. But don't pretend to be something you are not. Be who you are, all the time. And expect that from the people in your life. No more Jekyll and Hyde types allowed in your world, or mine. Only accept those who are real, who are true and allow them to be who they are. Not everyone in this world is good, and that is the way of the world. Let them be as they are, see them for what they are and either make the decision to accept it, look past it or walk away from it.

People are very inclined to set moral standards for others, but often disinclined to set them for themselves. Never trust the one whose deeds and whose talk do not match, trust your gut and know that while you will never change them, you do not have to be changed by them either. Be who you are, the good and the bad all the time, and only allow those into your life who are the same way. Learn to see people as they really are and not as they would have you believe. The hypocrite's life is a lonely existence, and only when they truly see themselves for what they are - will they be forced to make their own decision to change or not.

Burn, Baby, Burn

My Past:
I can choose to let it define me, confine me, refine me, outshine me...
or I can choose to move on and leave it behind me.

A while back I posted a picture on my Facebook fan page that was a piece of paper with the words: **"The Past"** written on it. The corner of the piece of paper was burning brightly. I captioned this picture with - *"Face it. Learn from it. Make peace with it. Then let it go."* The response was immediate and overwhelming. One lady called it the most empowering picture she had seen. Something so simple, yet so huge to most. You can't erase your past. Your history. It is there, will always be there. But what it doesn't always have to have, is a strangle hold on you. Over the years, I have done a number of times what this picture portrays. There is something so cathartic about fire. It cleanses. It's putting everything into a box and burning it. The finality like a slamming door. It can no longer hurt you; you have burned away its power over you. It is done.

We all have histories. No one makes it through life unscathed. It's a fact of life. Shit happens and you deal. But you can find ways to release its hold on you. The past is just that, past. It's over. Going over and over it in your head just means you can't or won't let it go. To some it is like a safety net, an excuse not to be happy, not to be confident or not to live. Instead of learning from it, facing it once and for all and eventually making peace with it. They hold it close. Almost like a barrier against anything worse happening. Or some use their past as a defense- It happened once, it could happen again. But when you do this, you lose your today.

Your today is the most important thing.

Your past: You can choose to let it define you, confine you, refine you, outshine you or you can choose to move on and leave it behind you. There is usually nothing tangible that you have to hold on to. However, maybe you have kept journals, a memory box, letters, or emails. Keeping anything that holds you to something you really need to let go of, will never release its hold on you and your life, until you find your power and strength to release them.

Use that one foot you have planted in the past to propel yourself forward to your future.

Burn it. Write things that you need to let go on a piece of paper. Write it all out of your system. Print off the emails and than burn them. A few months back I had a letter. It was a long letter that to me felt as solid as an anchor around my neck. Those seven pieces of paper had the weight of an albatross. Words. Powerful words that I never wanted to read again, but somehow couldn't stop. One day I had enough. I got a big steel pot, went outside and I burned that damn letter. I cried, I yelled and then I felt this calm. I had released something that had such a hold over me. I felt free, I felt lighter. I felt that I could finally get a handle on things and move out from underneath them. The feeling of setting those papers on fire and watching them burn and smoke was amazing.

I didn't walk away from burning that letter simply over the pain. When I walked away from that ceremonial burning though I was somehow, cleansed. That in burning it and scattering the ashes far away from me, I gave myself permission to move forward.

We will never forget our histories. The people who made appearances both good and bad. People we love and lost. Hurts we felt or inflicted. Mistakes we made. Time will never erase it, it will never disappear. But its hold, its power over you, will. You have the ultimate control over it. Use it. Feel that strength. Be bold.

Face it. Learn from it. Make peace with it. Then let it go.

Burn, Baby, Burn.

The Power of "No"

Believe in yourself enough to fight for you.
When you respect yourself, your time and your life,
others will have no choice but to respect it as well.

There is only one person you can count on 100% in this world to stand up for you, fight for you and demand respect for you. That is you. You have to plant your feet firmly, use your strongest voice and lay the law down. Only you. No one else has that power, as they shouldn't.

You wield all the power over your own existence. If you don't, then you are doing something wrong. Allowing people to walk all over you, make unrealistic demands of you, place their burdens on your shoulders instead of carrying their own load, has got to stop. You can give and give to people, however if they never once lift a hand to help themselves, it will never stop.

You will end up annoyed, exhausted and resentful. Thing is, you should be annoyed, at yourself. Not them. Really. Because you never once said "no", or stood by a "no" when you said it. You did and did some more until it became habit. You then get resentful because you are constantly doing, looking the other way or shouldering responsibilities that weren't yours to begin with, but are now, because you took them. You get tired of always being the one to do things. You get so exasperated that you want to throw your hands up and yell, *"No More!!"* But you never do.

Why is just saying "no", so hard? We all want to help people, be there for our friends and family. Why is setting boundaries with people we care about so impossible? Why is it so difficult to stand up for ourselves with family and friends? Is it because you are afraid that they will stop loving you? Walk away from you? Be mad at you? So what if they are? There is a lot of power in that phrase right there. *"So what?"* Let them be mad at you, let them walk away. Because doing so gives you your life back. They don't have to like it. Their happiness is not your responsibility. YOUR happiness is. They don't have to like it. But they have to respect it. You have to demand that they respect it. You have to-HAVE TO - stand up for yourself. Stand your ground and be firm.

Be your own champion. You don't need someone else to do it for you. You do it. You take control and stop letting people, family - whoever walk all over you. It's not OK. Stop justifying their behavior. You cannot help someone who will NOT help themselves. And they will never help themselves if you won't let them.

Getting angry at people who take advantage of you is easy. But looking internally and accepting the responsibility for allowing it, is not. You allowed it to happen. You took everything they handed you. Out of guilt, out of fear or lack of confidence, you took it. Seeing this for what it is should show you that you have control. You can say no, you just have to allow yourself. The world won't end. The sky won't fall. People may get mad; they may yell and carry on. That is up to them. They are responsible for their own lives. Regardless of how much you put into it. Give them the chance to live, to make mistakes, to become strong in their own right. By standing up for yourself, by saying no, you are giving them a gift. Though chances are they won't see it as such at first, or at all. But you will.

Take back the power of your life. Learn to stand up for yourself. Walk away if you have to; schedule alone time or me time. Understand that the only way people can take advantage of you, is if you allow it.

Believe in yourself enough to fight for you. If you respect you, your time and your life, others will have no choice but to respect it as well.

Pot Holes and Dark Clouds

I may not know where my road leads or what is around the next turn.
I may not see the sudden pot holes or dark clouds gathering.
I do know that I will continue walking - overcoming all that I find.
I will walk with humor and love. I will never lose my stride.

Recently, I came upon a crossroad that wasn't on any map in my world. Never saw it coming and then BAM! it was there. Rocked me pretty good. I thought that I may have finally come up against something that I wasn't prepared to handle. For me, this is unthinkable. I have faced and handled so much in my life, I was feeling pretty strong. Until I hit this particular crossroad, with dark storm clouds gathering off in the distance.

I stumbled a bit a first. The weight of what could happen took my breath away and felt like the pressure of the universe sat squarely on my shoulders. Still does. Except now I am in a holding pattern, as the direction I need to go in has not been revealed yet. Life has decided to take the wait and see approach to this particular event. To say I am not exactly pleased is an understatement. However I have absolutely zero control. So what am I going to do, wail at the heavens, plead with the stars? Not my style. I am going to dig deep and I am going to handle it. Whatever "it" turns out to be.

Life can deal some nasty blows and throw some very unpleasant surprises at you. It is up to you to see things for what they are and deal. You have to deal. You may stumble and feel like the weight of whatever you have in your life is going to crush you, but it won't. It may feel like your world is splitting apart at the seams that the pressure is going to drive you to your knees. It may. For a moment. That is ok. But only a moment. There was one moment during this "event" that I really was splintering. I wanted to run, I wanted to hide, I wanted to find someone and say, *"Here, you handle this. I can't."* I went outside and I stood real still. Inside I was waging a war with myself. There was no *"it will be OK"* or *"everything happens for a reason."* What happened was a knock down drag out fight with myself. I wanted to curl up in a little ball and hide. I stumbled. Ohhh hell did I. For a moment. It was like I had to release all that in order to get it out of my head to realize, I got this shit handled. Regardless of the outcome, regardless that it is completely out of my control. I will handle it. I will hope and pray for the best, but I will prepare for the worst. Because that is what you have to do. You dig deep, deeper still and you find that never-ending well of resolve to see what you have in front of you through. You don't back down, you don't walk away and you don't pretend it isn't there. You face it, you struggle with it and you handle it.

Life is messy. It is also wonderful, powerful and amazing. A bad moment in your life isn't your entire life. A bad year or two does not define your existence. Unless you let it. You can wallow in all that is wrong, or has been wrong. Piss and moan about all you have been through in the past, having going on today and could have in the future. Or you can see it for what it is. Do not let the pot holes of life define you. Let your strength and resolve to handle your business and get on with living be what defines you. You are strong enough, tough enough, and smart enough. Stop telling yourself otherwise. And above all else, you are worth it. You deserve all the happiness and love this life has to offer. But it is up to you to make it happen.

Walk your road with purpose. With your shoulders pulled back and a tilt to your chin. Look the world square in the eye and say; "I got this shit handled." Keep walking because you never know what is around that next bend, it could just be all that you wanted, dreamed of and wished for.

It Started As a Bad Hair Day...

It started as a bad hair day and went to hell from there.

Everything feels off. You are cranky and the crazy in the world seems to be following you everywhere you go. You glance at the sky to see if it is a full moon; you read your horoscope, sure that it will tell you should have stayed in bed. You get that feeling in your belly, tightness in your chest and that half a headache that just won't go away. You feel like you are running and running and then realize, yeah you have been running - just in circles. Days when no amount of coffee seems to perk you up and all you want to do is hide from the world. Yeah, it's been one of those days.

The type of day when everything that could go wrong, does. The days when a normally punctual you is late for everything, including getting up on time and out the door. Days where the coffee shop screws up the same order you have gotten for the past five years and where everyone on the road decided overnight that NASCAR moved the races to the highway and you are now in the Sprint Cup whether you wanted to be or not. You get cut off left and right, always seeming to have some guy riding your bumper. Yeah, been one of those days.

See it all started as a bad hair day and went to hell from there. I should have known what kinda day it would be really. Raining for the third day in a row. Totaling over seven inches of rain since the weekend. Ah hell, make that four days. See, it's one of those days when I don't even know what day of the week it is. Sigh. I think everyone I came into contact today was off, crazy or just simply weird. I realized around 3 pm that it really wasn't just me. Everyone was cranky, touchy and a pain in my ass. Ok, so I may be generalizing here a bit, but you get my meaning right? For no particular reason either. I slept good last night, did not have anything major pressing today, aside from the stress of a life situation I have going on, nothing to make me particularly bitchy today... but alas, I am. Locked into bitch mode and absolutely no justification for it.

Thing is - it happens. You have off days. It's not the end of the world. Well, it could be for someone who pisses me off. Just kidding. Sort of.

But I mean really, you are allowed to have one of those days once in a while. Its called being human. Days when the last thing you want to do is deal with any sort of crisis, ignorant person, well to be honest people in general. Days when you want to get home as fast as you can, get into comfy clothes and just be. I am normally not a negative person, but on days like today, I have learned not to fight it. I do what needs to be done and I head to the one place that never fails to soothe me. Home. I read a book and get lost in a story. I write. I create pictures and posters for my Facebook page or a zone out and watch TV. Anything to shut my brain off and get back to being Jenn. I am not going to sweat it. It happens. I have learned throughout my life that you need to listen to that little voice inside your head. If it is telling you the world has gone mad and that you need to go home and hide from the craziness, then do it.

Tomorrow is a new day. Let's hope my hair behaves.

Patchwork Memories

There has to come a time in your life when you make peace with
something that you will never be able to explain nor understand.
When you feel the broken pieces inside you come together.
Not in the same form as before it was broken.
But a new form.
A new piece to your soul that you carry on with.

I have had a memory montage playing in my head today. Off and on at random times. Stills flashing one right after another. All starring my mom. Some of the images have a sepia color to them, an aged appearance. Memories from long ago. Some are newer, fresher. Some of them have accompanying audio. Flashes of conversations had, music and laughter. I focus today on that, the laughter. The silliness. The jokes. The happy. There are two particularly prominent montages. In both of them, she has the same expression on her face. A twinkle in her eye and the appearance of completeness.

I am sitting on the front porch of our house. It sometime in the late 90's. The sun is shinning and there are big poofy white clouds in the sky. The colors of the surrounding trees a rich green. The lawn lush and full. I hear the deep guttural sound of a motorcycle off in the distance. As the sound gets louder I look down the street. Motorcycles were not really common in our neighborhood. I look at this bike as it comes closer and I am stunned.

It is my mother. On a motorcycle! By herself. I find myself rooted to the ground as I stare in wonder. Not so much at the fact of her riding the bike. But simply the expression on her face. Gone were the worry lines. Gone was the sadness. Her eyes lost that haunted look and were shinning. She was smiling - really smiling. For the first time in my memory she looked free. The pride she had in that moment. The strength and the happy, will forever been burned into my memory. She had found something in life finally that had given it to her. The freedom she had longed for. She rode that bike like she had been doing it for years. Each time with that same expression. When she rode, her mind cleared. It was her, the bike and the open road. It settled her. It made her happy. For a brief moment in time she held on to that.

The second memory comes a few years later. The time with the bike had abruptly come to an end. She no longer wanted it. She suddenly decided to sell it. The period that followed was a long one for her. Back was the haunted look, the smile that never really reached her eyes. Until one day she decided to buy a new car. She was spontaneous at times. Suddenly getting an idea in her head and jumping on it. I will never forget this day either.

She went off and traded in her SUV. She came home that day with a brand new, fuchsia Mustang convertible. She had that same expression on her face. Looking back now I understand it more. Both the motorcycle and the convertible gave her the one thing in life she needed most. Freedom. Wind in your hair, speeding down the road with no destination in sight and no where to be. She would turn the music up loud, turn her mind down and just drive. Her face would clear, worry lines fade and she would smile. Really smile. Though it never lasted. For a brief moment in time she was happy.

Today I do not want to focus on the fact that she is gone. I don't want to feel the sadness, nor the anger. I do not want to focus on anything but the good. The singing made up lyrics to songs as we drove around in that convertible. Banging on closed doors as we went by to illicit a scream of surprise followed by uncontrollable laughter. How she called me kid even when I was well beyond. How she found peace on her riding lawn mower of all places. How she was to strangers she met and the random acts of kindness she would do. How when she was working at the Maine Gift store we had for years, she would hide little trinkets in the bags of customers who were having a hard day.

Today I want to remember her with that look she had on her face the day she came home on her motorcycle. Happy. Content. Free. So alive. I want to remember the laughter. For today I want to lock away the memories of her illness. I want the memory montages to be of happy times. I want to feel the warmth of those times.

Had my mom made the decision to live, she would be 58 today. Though impossible to send her birthday wishes, I still find myself sitting on my deck, faced turned to the sun and sending her wishes of peace. Of freedom. I wish with everything I have that she is now content. Though no longer of this world, she will always be of us. In our memories. In our lives and in our hearts. For today, this is what I hold on to. Maybe as a birthday gift to her, it is what I will hold on to forevermore.

There has to come a time in your life when you make peace with something that you will never be able to explain nor understand. When you feel the broken pieces inside you come together. Not in the same form as before it was broken. But a new form. A new piece to your soul you carry on with. Maybe today that is what I give her for her birthday. I scatter all the broken pieces around. Pick and chose the ones that mean the most. Create a new piece that fits into the hole she left. Choosing pieces of memories that show her at her best. Put the pieces together and make sense out of something that on its own never will.

This will be my birthday present to her. A patchwork of memories that lives inside my soul. That will always be a part of me. Filing that hole she left with love, humor and a part of her soul. It feels peaceful to me when I look up at the sky now. The sun shines alittle brighter.

I make a silent birthday wish to her, a secret whisper.

Get Your Big Girl Panties On

Sometimes life is messy. It knocks you down, breaks your heart and kicks you around for good measure. This is when you just gotta get your big girl panties on and deal with it.

Did you know that it is OK to get mad? That it is OK to get frustrated, sad, and lonely? That there will be days in your lifetime that you just won't be able to find your happy? Has anyone ever told you that this is OK? Most when they get tired and frustrated tell themselves to *"shake it off"* or *"get over it."* Or even worse - someone else tells them to *"Just get over it."* They deny these very pressing feelings because they don't think they should allow them room in their day.

A lot of people simply press these feelings down inside and bury them. In reality all this does is cause them to build up and fester. By not dealing with them and letting them out at the time, all you are doing is making things worse in the long run. Denying them does not make them disappear.

You can slap a smile on your face and even convince others you are happy. But you know. Somewhere inside you realize that in truth you are anything but. There is a phrase that makes me cringe every time I read it. *"Fake it til you make it."* As if you can fake happiness. Why in the world would you even want to? Wouldn't you rather pull those feelings you have been denying out, face them and deal with them AND then get on to the business of loving life?

Sometimes life is messy. It knocks you down, breaks your heart and kicks you around for good measure. By not allowing yourself time to get your mad on, your sad on or your *"holy hell, I hate the world"* on, you will never get past it. It is like dressing it up, putting some cover up on it and hoping to fool not only the world, but yourself. It just doesn't work. Well, maybe for a time. But there will be something that triggers you and probably the smallest thing ever. But something will trigger you and you will no longer be able to control it. Your negative will then control you. Honestly, it will probably be 100 times harder to deal with later on. If you allow all the "crap" to percolate and to grow, it always seems to get 300% worse than it was initially. By not allowing these emotions to flow out of you, giving them the time they deserve. You are in essence giving them control over your mind and your soul. Even if you tell yourself you are happy, you can't fake yourself out forever. And it will probably be the poor kid that screwed up your coffee order that will get your wrath.

I am just jaded enough not to trust someone who is happy all the time. Who radiates sunshine and smiles where ever they go? These are usually the ones I really worry about. The truth of the matter is sometimes life can be a bitch.

Thing is, you can be a bitch right back. This is OK! Gasp!

There I said it. It is in writing. If you are feeling frustrated, angry and overwhelmed or sad. Deal with it! Right then. Or as soon as you can get sometime to yourself. Get it out of you as fast as you can. Put on your big girl (or boy) panties and face it. Give yourself time to be anything but happy. Just don't let it consume you. In reality, denying them as valid, not giving yourself permission to let them flow out of you. They will consume you. They will force themselves out whether you want them to or not. You retain all ultimate control over them as long as you deal with them and let it happen. If you keep pushing them down inside you, to some back corner of "you." You relinquish all control and hand the reins over. Whether you even realize it or not.

Thing is, there are probably some very valid reasons why you have got your sad on, your mad on, your frustrated on in the first place. Something or someone has caused this to happen. Chances are these emotions have built up and built up over time. Most days it takes a lot to make me angry or mad. Granted there are certain triggers, people mostly, that can make me go zero to bitch mode really quickly. But I have learned to just let these emotions happen. They end on their own. I either walk it off, think about it some or occasionally I will write about it. Anything to get it out of me. I don't have time for it.

Some days I get sad. Revelation? No, not really. Everyone does. Maybe something will trigger a memory of a time past, loved one lost or a life event will happen and make me sad. I let it. There are good positive emotions and there are not so positive emotions. Each needs room in your world for a time. You will be surprised how free you feel if you just let them roll.

I know it's not PC to tell you that it's OK to get mad or sad or whatever. But it is reality. Some days there will be something that really gets to you. Don't deny yourself this. Identify what made you feel this way. Let your mind flow. Understand yourself and figure out why you reacted the way you did.   Or if it is a situation that consistently happens or something that keeps rearing it's ugly head. This is life trying to tell you it is something you HAVE GOT to deal with. Stop denying yourself the release.

Think about it. Break it down. Put on those big girl panties and deal with it. Then and only then, let it go. Be free of it.   Then go back and get your happy on :)

Face Meet Palm

Sometimes in life the only response is a facepalm.
For some things there are just no words.

We have all had this experience. For some of us it is a daily occurrence. That moment in your day when you are forced to deal with a situation or person and you find yourself totally and completely without words. They open their mouth to speak, do something so ignorant; that the only proper response is a facepalm. Usually a facepalm is accompanied by a slight shaking of the head and a closing of the eyes. A brief respite in time when one hopes that when one opens one's eyes, the cause of said facepalm has either disappeared or magically became intelligent.

Never works.

Words are my thing. Snappy comebacks and sarcastic retorts, second nature. But there are days when even I am at a loss. It tends to be the same people over and over again who force me to introduce my palm to my face. Occasionally a stranger or someone I come across in my day will elicit one. But it is normally the usual suspects. People that make me want to shout at the top of my lungs -**"Reallllly?"** Followed by the urge to ask them how they survive the day. Snarky. I know. But some people seriously bring it out. I feel like you are reading this and laughing. You have a face palmer too, don't ya?

These people consistently make my days seem to last so much longer. They make my head hurt. I question how they made it this far. Normally the type of person who causes a facepalm tends to view themselves as intelligent, witty and well - right. All the time. They concoct ideas, views and arguments. They get in your face and tell you all the reasons that they are right. You look at them, cock your head sideways and think to yourself, I hear sounds coming out of your mouth but I think you sound like the teacher from Charlie Brown... WaaawaaaWaaWaaa Waa. They walk away and you are forced to do it. Face meet palm.

If you are lucky you can find humor in these situations. I know some people who make me facepalm all the time. One in particular. There is no humor there. Well sometimes I will laugh at this particular person. I am actually afraid to open my mouth. *(Sometimes that brain - to - mouth filter of mine doesn't work so well.)* I often want to call out the cause of my facepalm. But figure it's a waste of words, of breath and well - thought processes.

May you get through the rest of your week without having to introduce your face to your palm. I know. I know. Wishful thinking. But you can at least shake your head and find the humor in it.

Paying It Forward

That best portion of a good man's life; His little, nameless,
unremembered acts of kindness and of love.
William Wordsworth (1770-1850)

There really is no small act of kindness. Even the smallest act can have a profound impact on the life of another.

Awhile back I was in a convenience store. It was a busy Saturday and there were a ton of customers. Each in a hurry to get to their weekend festivities. One lone sales clerk ran the register. As the line grew longer and longer you could see her stress level growing. She wasn't deaf to the grumblings of the people as they waited.

One guy needed ice, which was locked up outside. When I walked in he was outside waiting for her to come out to unlock the bin. He followed me as I walked inside the store. I glanced back at him when I heard him bark at the girl that he had been waiting four minutes and he wanted his ice. He yelled at her, "Now Dammit!" and stormed back out. I grabbed my coffee and went and stood in line. At this point there was on three people in front of me. When it became my turn, I looked at her and gave a small smile. I told this poor kid that I was in no hurry and I would wait for her to go take care of the guy with the ice. The guy behind me grumbled and I fix him with a glare. She smiled gratefully and ran outside.

When she came back, she had tears in her eyes. She said I had no idea what gift I had just given her. She wanted to hug me. Really, all I did was wait an extra two minutes. That small gesture meant the world to her. Out the door I went. When I stopped in yesterday I was greeted by a giant smile. Same clerk. She whispered to her co-worker as I walked by; *"that is the lady I told you about."* That small act cost me nothing.

I remember once a few years back my kid and I were walking into the supermarket. There was this adorable little old lady loading her bags into her trunk. She was just putting the last bag in and her carriage was empty. My kid walked over to her, smiled took the carriage from her and said, "I'll return it. Have a nice day." This little old lady looked at him and awarded him with the biggest smile. She looked at me and winked.

That small completely random act of returning her carriage for her made her day. I was so proud of my kid. When I told him that, he just looked at me, shrugged and asked if we could get Cheerios for cereal.

There are opportunities everywhere to touch someone's life. Everyday they are there. It's just so easy to get caught up in the craziness of life, that we miss the chances.

When I created the Random Thoughts page on Facebook I had no idea what would come of it. Over time, I have had the pleasure to network with other Facebook pages and their creators and was invited to join a group for inspirational page owners. A forum to discuss our work, our ideas, issues that arise and ways we can touch the most people possible. In this group are people from all over the world, who every day dedicate their time and energy into putting positive, uplifting messages into the world. For no other reason than because they can. They want to make people think, feel inspired and laugh. They want people to feel less alone.

One woman in particular, has touched my heart. Her name is Carmen and she is the creator behind the Facebook page called "Paying It Forward ~ One Day at a Time." Her whole goal is to inspire people to reach out in kindness to someone and for that someone to pay it forward to another. In a world filled with strife. Where the evening news is all about loss, devastation, wars and all the bad. This woman wants to trump all that, by spreading kindness.

Simple, really, when you think about it.

Carmen even created little bright green bracelets that *say "Paying It Forward ~ One Day at a Time"* on it. The magic behind these bracelets is awesome. While sitting in my truck the other day waiting to get my coffee I had an idea. When it was my turn at the window, I told the guy I wanted to pay for the woman behind me as well. I gave him one of the green bracelets and asked that he give it to her with her coffee and tell her I said "Happy Thursday." Off I went about my day. Quite frankly, it made me feel good to do it. I love the little secret acts that one can do everyday. Especially when the receiver has no idea who you are or where you come from.

Sometimes when my family and I go out to dinner, we will pick someone who is dining alone. We ask our server to put their dinner on our bill, but not to say anything to them. We giggle at our mischievousness. We pay the bill and scurry out of the restaurant. We could be having the worst day ever, but in that small random act it turns our whole day around.

Practice random acts of kindness. Open the door for a stranger. Help someone with their groceries. Kindness costs nothing, but is priceless. Strangers, friends and family. Start small. One random off - the – cuff - act a day. Go get some of your own Paying It Forward bracelets and give them out. Leave them with your tip at dinner for the stressed out server with a note telling them "Thanks." Tape a dollar to a vending machine with a note that says, "Next One on Me. Pay it Forward."

Keep your eyes open.
There will be a chance every day to: "Pay It Forward."

Mirror Mirror on the Wall

In truth it is not even really about you. It has always been about them.
Their issues and their hang ups. You are just fine the way you are.
Remember that.

Have you ever seen the *"Wizard of Oz," "Snow White"* or the TV show *"Once Upon a Time?"* At the heart of each one of these is good vs. evil-bad vs. good. Throughout the story the battle goes back and forth until you are left on the edge of your seat wondering who is ahead and who is behind. You curse when the Bad scores points against the Good and cheer when Good prevails. Back and forth it goes in constant drama. Makes for good television, but not so much when you are faced with it in life. Maybe not evil per se, but the back and forth with someone that only wants to hurt, discredit or force you to eat the poisoned apple.

When someone is so full of pain, of insecurity or just plain miserable with their own lives, they tend to lash out at others. Hoping to elevate their own conditions, they force a power play of sorts. Breaking another down as a way of building themselves up. If it goes on for a long period of time, it becomes habit for this type of person. It eats even further away at what good they had inside.

It becomes all encompassing and a way of life. Lash out at someone who they perceive as better, happier more successful and in turn they feel better about themselves. A slight twist of reality and Poof! Like magic, they are better than the one they have been focusing on. Their negativity seeps through though unrealized and touches everything around them. Plunging them further into the darkness. They will continually lash out because they lack the strength to take a honest look at their own lives. It becomes an obsession of sorts.

Take the Wicked Witch in Oz. She stalked Dorothy. She sent flying monkeys at her; she threatened her and did everything to exert her power over her. Green with jealously; locked in her castle, she needed to hurt what was good. She manipulated and lied and looked for any opening to release her pain onto another. It is the same with this type of person. They never realize their actions will not lead to a better life. Nor do they seem to care. For as long as they are focusing on the actions of another, they need not be looking at themselves.

I feel sorry for people like this. Who lack the strength to fix their own lives. That allow their unhappiness to direct the course their lives take. The pain and heartache they can inflict on others is a direct reflection back on them. But one they will avoid seeing at all costs. They lie. They bully. They lash out. They talk behind your back and do whatever they can to discredit you. They keep files and notes and look for whatever opening they can find to hurt you. They infiltrate your friends, your family and your life. But only if you allow it. You do not have to let their poison effect you.

In truth it is not even really about you. It has always been about them. Their issues, their hang ups. Nothing you could ever do or say will change it. When you realize this, the power shifts. Hold your head up high, shoulders back and remember that it is not your battle to fight, you do not ever need to defend yourself. Because the fight is inside of them. They need to make peace with themselves.

Maybe if you are lucky they will manipulate themselves into $20,000 that they can put towards therapy.

But, I wouldn't eat any apples in the meantime.

Tailgate Wisdom

I am fluent in four languages. English, sarcasm, profanity and Male.
It was the last one that was the hardest to master.

The other day, a good friend of mine stopped by. Randomly out of the blue. I happened to be sitting on my deck having coffee and writing, as it was early morning. I glanced up as I heard the deep guttural sound of a souped - up exhaust. As he got out of his huge truck - coffee in hand, I knew something was up. My usually smiling, happy – go - lucky friend looked forlorn, lost and sad. You have to get a picture of this guy in your head. He is tall, strong as an ox and a man's man. Rugged and tough on the outside, big teddy bear on the inside. But he is a guy. With obvious guy tendencies.

Talking isn't one of his strong points. So when he shows up out of the blue, with coffee and a lost look on his face, I knew something was up. I also knew it was going to be an hour and several cups of coffee before he got around to it. Thankfully, I am multilingual. I speak English, sarcasm, profanity, and "Male." Being fluent in Male comes in handy at times like these.

After about the fifth cup of coffee and the latest news on his truck modifications, he finally had gotten around to the reason behind his visit. He had an argument with his girlfriend the night before. He knew that he had screwed something up, but was unable to translate her words into Male. So he came to see me.

Once the caffeine had loosened his tongue, he got into the gist of the argument. Apparently there had been a discussion on soul mates. She had made a comment about a girlfriend of hers finding her soul mate. My friend, sensing he was supposed to contribute something, said that was awesome for her. He knew how awesome it was to find his soul mate. He had her. In his world, this comment was the type to score some brownie points. And thing is, he really means it. But then, he followed it up with, *"finding your soul mate is cool, it takes the pressure off and you don't have to work at it any more. You find the one you are supposed to love and that's it."*

Apparently his girlfriend took exception to the follow up comment. Her rebuttal was something along the lines of; "Of course you still have to work at it. You have to show the person you love, how much they mean to you. Actions, speak louder than words." There was a lot more she said - a lot more. But the basic summary is, she now understands why he never goes that extra effort for her, does special things just for her or puts any thought into their relationship. He thinks he is done. He has her, he is happy and now doesn't need to worry or think about it anymore. If only right?

I thought for a moment. Here is this awesome guy. He loves his girlfriend, plans on marrying her soon. He doesn't want anyone else. He is happy. He is also now seriously confused. I got up from my chair and told him to follow me. I walked over to his truck and started speaking Male.

I opened the little door to his gas tank and said *"What goes in here?"* He replied fuel. Then I popped the hood. I pointed to the spark plugs and said, *"What are these for?"* He replied that they were spark plugs and that they caused the spark to ignite the fuel. No spark. No combustion. No combustion. No go. He is glaring at me now because he knows I know all of this and thinks I am toying with him. Then I point to the oil cap and say *"Why does your truck need oil?"* He replied through gritted teeth, that it lubricates the engine components and makes it run smoothly. Now he is really looking at me like I have finally lost it. So I drop the tailgate, sit down and say...

"You put fuel in twice a week. The spark plugs ignite the fuel and cause combustion. This causes you to go. The oil lubricates all your engine components and makes things run smoothly. This takes maintenance. This takes thought. This takes work. You forget to maintain anyone of these and your truck breaks down. The same thing goes for your relationship. You are the fuel, your love is the spark plug and the oil, well the oil is the blood and life of your relationship. You have to maintain the oil, just like you have to maintain your life. Your actions fuel your relationship, your thoughts spark it and your love makes it run smoothly. If any one of these breaks down, you have to fix it in order for it to work. Routine maintenance is key."

He stood very still. His eyes looking at his truck but seeing in his mind his girlfriend. He understood. He works hard, he is always faithful and he loves her. But what he didn't realize at first is that while all of this was the fuel to his relationship he still needed to maintain it. He still needed to make that special effort for her. For her and him. It was only together that their engine ran smoothly. Now he understood that not only did he need to remember to get gas and his oil changed. He also needed to dedicate time and attention to her. She wasn't the type who needed a big display or expensive gifts and he knew that. He also knew that he was going to do whatever it took to make her happy.

He looked at me with a grin and said he was going home to tell her that he understood. That she was just like his truck and he was going to treat her the same way. I just shook my head at him and let him go. Baby steps. She will understand. He is a guy after all.

To Each Their Own

There will always be someone different than you. That is what makes the world such an amazing place and life such an amazing journey. Each one of us has a place in this world. The time has come to accept this. The time has come to evolve once again.

Growing up my grandmother always taught me that it is what a person has on the inside that counts. That it didn't matter what color they were, what church they belonged to or how much they made. What made a person worth knowing you had to look for, listen for and feel. That just because someone drove a fancy car, had the best of everything or went to church every Sunday, didn't show me anything more about them, then how they chose to spend their money or their Sunday.

You learn about people through their actions. If you saw good in them, believe it. If you saw bad, believe that too. Always be true, be fair and give people the benefit of the doubt.

She also taught me that every person in this world deserves to be here. That I didn't necessarily have to believe in them, agree with them or even like them. But they deserve to be here as much as I. She taught me values. She taught me open mindedness. She taught one other powerful lesson: Treat others as I want them to treat me. Well I have grown up and I still hold these truths as a guide to live my life by. I don't care if you are rich or poor, black or white, Catholic, Christian or atheist. I don't care if you make a boatload of money, sweep floors or flip burgers. I do not care if you are educated or not. I do not care if you are gay, straight, bi or single and getting it where you can. All I care about is who you are as a person and how you treat others. What do you give out to the world? Who are you on the inside?

When I see people in my community, my state or this nation hate on a specific group of people because they are different than them, it makes me crazy. Just because someone is different than you does not make you a better person. It just makes you different. Differences are awesome. Can you imagine how boring life would be if we were all the same? Seriously. I can't imagine a world where every one looked like me, talked like me thought like me. It would be so boring. But yet, every time I turn on the news or read a paper this is what I see. Wars, fighting, demonstrations. One side versus the other side. Each side claiming they are right, that their way is the only way. Really? Just because something isn't right for one makes it wrong for all? Just because I eat meat doesn't make me a horrible person. It makes me someone who eats meat. Just because you go to a Catholic church and your neighbor worships in a small Baptist chapel, doesn't make you right and him wrong. It makes you Catholic and him a Baptist. Both human beings, both good people. Just different. Just because I chose to love and marry a man doesn't make me any better than the man who marries another man. I am right for me. He is right for him. Simple as that. Or at least it should be.

Human beings have always formed "family units" in order to survive. When a father passed along the protection of his daughter to another man, marriage was created to formalize the agreement. In essence the woman was property. The agreement for marriage usually came with some form of financial arrangement. A dowry was often given to the husband for taking care of his wife.

In return, the wife had no rights to any of their property or children. She also had no right to refuse sex at any time with her husband. If he wanted it, she had to give it to him or he would simply just take it. There was a time in certain areas of England, when wives were often sold between men. This was the crude creation of what is now called divorce. As a woman, I am so glad that we have evolved from this. That we as the human race have gotten to where we are today. I can't imagine being sold as property. I can't imagine not having the legal right to refuse sex to my husband.

We saw a need to protect our rights as women. That we own the rights to our bodies, our minds and share equal rights in raising our children and owning property. We now have the freedom to vote, to marry who we choose, and if we do not want to have sex, we aren't forced against our will because he is in the mood. Our rights have evolved. The men in various religious organizations fought it. We fought back. Why? Because no one should ever exert that much control over someone who can think, make decisions and has the basic human right to love whomever they chose.

Why, then, is this is the case with women and not with a gay or lesbian couple who want to marry? You do not have to like it. You do not have to participate in it. You can still believe your beliefs, still go to church and enjoy your freedom to do so. What we as a nation do not have is the right to do is deny these same freedoms to anyone else. Be they gay, straight or purple. What we have to do is respect it. Why? Because like the women of old, it is their right to own their own bodies, their own minds and their right to love whomever they choose.

You have the right to practice your religion. You have the right to pray and you have the right to disagree with their choices. You even have the right to voice your beliefs. What we shouldn't do though is convince ourselves that this gives us the right or the freedom to deny others the same courtesy.

If everyone just took a step back and freely gave these rights to others that they hold so close and cherish for themselves, we wouldn't have demonstrations at a friggin' fast food chicken restaurant. We could focus more on our own lives and ways to be better people, better and stronger families and a better race entirely.

There will always be someone different than you. That is what makes the world such an amazing place and life such an amazing journey. Each one of us has a place in this world. The time has come to accept this. The time has come to evolve once again. The time to give equal rights is now. I am not trying to change anyone's opinion. What you believe is right for you. I may agree with it or I may not. But I what I will never agree to is denying anyone their equal rights. As an American. As a human being. It really should just be a given.

That is what I have on the inside.

Don't Just Look...See

If you spend too much time making judgments and not seeing people for who they really are, it is you who will lose out. Finding inspiration in people you meet on a daily basis makes life so much more interesting. Everyone you come across in life is fighting some kind of battle. Maybe they can shed some light on yours.

You are in grocery store. Harried, stressed and exhausted. There is a woman in front of you, youngish - 40s maybe. She is walking exactly where you want to be, where you deserve to be. She is not walking fast enough. Not moving fast enough. You clear your throat loudly. Hoping she takes the hint.

You want to yell *"Move it or lose it sister!"* at the top of your lungs. She moves ahead a bit and slowly reaches for an item on the shelf. You feel your heart start to race, blood pressure go up. The urge to tap her with your carriage is overwhelming. You have to get home, you have dinner to make. You have laundry that needs to be finished. You have things to do. Clearing your throat didn't move her fast enough. You sigh. Loudly. She glances at you and smiles. A warm smile. She grabs her carriage and walks forward. Still not fast enough for you, but she is out of your way. You grab what you need and you are off. Zipping past her, dirty glance in her direction. The nerve. Some people. World revolves around them. As you reach the end of your shopping, you glance over and see that she has only made it another 4 aisles. You think she is lazy, checking prices because she is poor. You check out and you leave. Not giving her another thought. Places to go, things to do. You are normally a patient person. But seriously, if she lost some weight, got a better job or whatever her reason for being so slow, so in your way, she would have gone faster.

In the time span of a quick stop at the grocery store, you glanced at a woman briefly. You didn't actually see her. You didn't get a sense of her. All you saw was what you projected onto her. Lazy, slow, fat, poor. You tried and convicted her in the space of a minute. You felt better about yourself without even realizing it. Then you were gone.
What you didn't see - what you would have seen had you taken a moment. Only a moment and actually looked at her - was pain. Not in any outward signs, but in her face. In her walk. The way she maneuvered

her carriage, getting the item and getting out of your way. You didn't see her. But she sure as hell saw you.   She smiled at you. Knowing full well your anger at her. She smiled. Until you walked past. Then the hurt set in.

There are 50 million Americans, one in five, who suffer from an autoimmune disease.   26.2% of Americans, one in four, suffer from mental illness. 7.8% or 5.2 million Americans will suffer or suffer from PTSD (post traumatic stress disorder). All of these show no outward symptoms. Nothing you would see at a quick glance.   But each one is like an albatross hanging around the neck of the person who suffers from it. That woman in the grocery store was trying. Trying to be independent. Trying to live through the pain. Each step she took sent shock waves through her. But she was determined. Determined not to let her disease stop her from living. She did it. She did her own shopping. This is a natural thoughtless act for most, for her it was an act of sheer strength and determination. But one that no one sees.

Every day you walk past people and automatically judge them. It is a human trait. You see what you want to see, what you are conditioned to see and you judge. Probably not even realizing you are doing it at the time. Everyone is so busy. So caught up in their own little world that we fail to see what is often right in front of us. We judge. We sigh loudly at the slow shopper. We tell the overweight person to exercise more, not understanding it is their medication that makes them that way. We tell the man who can't work, can't function to get over his depression. Just be happy already. People just don't get it. They don't see it and when they do actually see it, they turn their heads and are thankful it isn't them. They judge in order to distance themselves from it.

These people who suffer from diseases you can't see are so impressive to me. They work; they get up everyday knowing what is in store for them. They do it any way. They strive for independence and they try so hard not to let the world see just how hard it is. They lean on those close to them and try not to feel the guilt that it causes. They take medications that make them sick, but are up every morning with their kids. They try. By sheer force of will they make a life for themselves. They are strong, they are tough and they understand that when their disease puts limitations on them, it's time to find a way to work around it. They do it everyday. For some people getting up and out of bed is a victory. Grocery shopping is a cause for celebration. Going fishing and spending time alone for the first time in years, life changing.

I was talking to a friend awhile back. She suffers from an autoimmune disease. She went camping. Alone with her dog and her pistol. She sent her husband home. She reclaimed some of her independence. She fished, she cooked and cleaned. She was in constant pain but she did not let it stop her. She faced her disease and found ways to work around it. Her happiness and her strength were palpable. Without even realizing it she was inspiring.

We all have limitations. We all have something that stands in our way at times. We get frustrated, we cry and yell **"Why me?"** When what we should be doing is taking a page from my friend's book and say instead, *"What can I do different to get where I need to be?"*

Don't just look. See. If you spend too much time making judgments and not seeing people for who they really are, it is you who will lose out. Finding inspiration in people you meet on a daily basis makes life so much more interesting. Everyone you come across in life is fighting some kind of battle. Maybe, just maybe, they can shed some light on yours.

Don't just look… **See**.

Own Your Needs

Own your needs. Own what makes you come alive. Defend them. Stand by them. Know yourself. Believe in yourself. Trust yourself.

Every human being has basic physical needs. Air, water, shelter and sustenance. These are physical needs we require to stay alive. But there is alive and then there is living. Our living needs are not that much more complicated or extensive. But they are important. Needs are very personal and different from one person to the next. Needs have to be met. Have to be. If they are not, than we need to figure out why and take steps to get them met.

Wants are a different animal. We all want for something. But the wants do not dictate our being alive nor our living. Our wants do not have to be met in order for us to be happy and content. Complete. Wants are the cherry on our sundae. We do not need the cherry but we want the cherry. We do not need a flat screen television, we want one. We do not need to be wealthy; we want the freedom it allows. Wants vs. Needs. Identifying them helps you to avoid living in a constant state of craving and disappointment.

How many times have you said to yourself - I will be happy when I_____*fill in the blank.* Get a new job. Lose 20 pounds. Have more money. Husband cleans more. Wife stops nagging. The list of what we think we require allowing ourselves to be content; has a potential of being endless. When I... After I... If only I... Say you lose 20 pounds, then what? POOF! You are living the life you dreamed? Probably not. You may be happy for a while then something else will be missing from your life and it will be back to the same on litany. When I. After I. If only I...

We all have needs. Irrevocable needs. Aside from what it takes to be alive - what makes you come alive? What do you need to be content-to be happy? If your needs go by the wayside day after day with you doing nothing to correct it - how will it ever get better?

You are the ONLY one responsible for your needs. Not your spouse. Not your children. Not your work. Just You. Never look to anyone or anything outside of your self to meet them. If you are in a relationship and your needs are consistently not being met and you have communicated clearly about them, then it is up to you to stay or go based on that. If you make the decision to stay and nothing changes - the responsibility for this is on you. It is no longer their fault.

You must make a conscious decision to create the life you need.

The big thing in life is having a clear understanding of the difference between want and need. You do not need your husband to shower you in gifts and come home every night with flowers. You need him to pay more attention to you as a woman. You need to feel connected. Important. Same thing goes for your husbands, ladies. They do not need for you to shower them in gifts - but they do need your undivided attention as well. Husbands need to feel important, wanted and connected too. This applies to all of your relationships. Friends, family and coworkers. If you are consistently not having your needs met in these relationships, then it is time to reassess. You are not required to sacrifice your happiness nor your needs in order to be a part of anything. It is OK to walk away. It is OK to stand up for yourself and say this is not healthy for me. This is not what I need.

Own your needs. Own what makes you come alive. Defend them. Stand by them. Know yourself. Believe in yourself. Trust yourself. Hard sometimes I know. But you are worth it.

Once your needs are met. Well then it is time to focus on getting that cherry on your sundae.

Only In Silence
Can You Hear

*Life often mimics the ocean. A constant ebb and flow. High tides and
low. Sometimes volatile and stormy or covered in a blanket of fog.
But it always finds its calm eventually.*

There are moments in life when you need to take a step back to gain
perspective. Sometimes it takes even more than just a step. Sometimes
you need to run away. Away from all the distractions, the memories and
the ghosts. Sometimes you need to step out of your comfort zone and
throw everything into the wind. Sometimes you need to just walk away.
Not forever. Just long enough for you to find the silence and the peace
you need in order to hear the thoughts inside of your own mind.

I lasted seven years.

I call it the seven-year chapter. Looking back from where I sit right now,
it felt like 20 but seems to have gone by in a blink. It wasn't all bad. I met
and married my best friend. I became a step mother. I lived and I loved.
There was some laughter and good times. But it was also to date - the
longest stretch of time in my life. I know each and every one of you
know the feeling. When the weight of the world lies squarely on your
shoulders. When the pressure mounts and you have no choice but to pick
up and carry on. A time in your life when you feel the walls closing in
and all you want to do is hide. But you don't. You continue on step by
step. Eyes always hopeful for that proverbial light at the end of the
tunnel. Some days taking even the smallest of steps seems impossible.

It is easy at times to develop coping measures. Throwing yourself into
work. Taking mental escapes into books. Making yourself so busy that
you are too exhausted at the end of the day to even think about things.
You master the art of busy work. Anything not to think. Really think.
You zone out watching movies. You listen to music. Anything to stop
your thoughts from going to places you really aren't ready to face. For
me - *well* - I work, I read, I write. I focus on everyone else who is going
through a hard time and I help them. I listen. I offer my shoulder and a
hand. I cope by taking care of others. Until recently when I realized
something. It was time to take care of myself. I had stayed in my comfort

zone long enough. I had run from one task to another and I was tired. So tired. No longer could I silence the thoughts in my head. I needed to give them room.

My seven-year chapter culminated the summer of 2012 when there was a chance my husband would be diagnosed with cancer. For five months we went from doctor to doctor. Two major surgeries and hurry – up - and - wait mentality. When we finally got the diagnosis that it was not cancer but another less scary issue, the weight of all that I had been carrying was just too much. I didn't break. But found that I could bend a lot more then I realized.

I scheduled some time off from work. I did not read a book, did not write anything and posted very little on the Random Fan Page. My husband and I packed our bags and just took off. No reservations. No clear path. Just away. I wanted peace and quiet and an ocean view. We ended up in Bar Harbor, Maine. Only three hours north of where we live but a world away. For two days we hiked in Acadia National Forest, we took a cruise around Frenchmen's bay and I let my thoughts go. I sat on our balcony and stared out to the ocean. It was in the early morning hours with the entire coast shrouded in dense fog that I felt something release inside of me. Calm descended in my scattered thoughts, my shoulders relaxed and I just let it all go. All the hurt. All the sadness. All the bad. It not longer deserves a place in my thoughts or my world. I just need the silence to hear it.

When the fog cleared and I could once more see the ocean again, I realized something. Life often mimics the ocean. A constant ebb and flow. High tides and low. Sometimes volatile and stormy or covered in a blanket of fog. But it always finds its calm eventually. Same thing goes for you and I. Life may have its share of storms and hard times. But it is a constant flow. We are not meant to stay safe on the shore and watch it pass us by. We were made to live it. All of it.

At some point our storms will pass and the fog will clear and we will eventually find our calm.

Random Life Lessons

Life can change for all of us in an instant.

I am always on the lookout for lessons. Always wondering what a chance encounter with a stranger is supposed to teach me. Always listening for little pearls of wisdom from children and the elderly. Always paying attention to each new person that enters my life - my little corner of the world, for when they share their experiences I often learn something new. Sometimes if I am lucky some random person will say something that sparks my thoughts and away I go.

Once or twice a month since his wife passed, he comes to see me. He makes his way slowly down the hall to my office and appears at my door. Stooped slightly with brilliant white hair and carrying his checkbook, he always looks at me sheepishly. He claims to have a question on his billing statement. But he knows that I know, it is just a ruse to come see me. This man was a doctor in his day and still carries about him that air of confidence. It is embedded in his soul. Until he comes into my office and lets his guard down. I can feel his sadness roll off him in waves. He misses his wife. But it is more than that. He is lost without her, literally and figuratively.

He spent 12 years earning his medical degree. Then decades building his practice and providing for his family. His wife ran the house, the children and all of the day - to - day tasks that he took for granted. With her gone now, he has no idea what to do. It confuses him, frightens him and makes him doubt himself. After a lifetime of healing others, to see a proud 78 – year - old man doubt himself gives me pause. So we talk.

This man - a doctor. Performed complicated surgeries. Held the very lives of his patients in his hands. Yet cannot begin to figure out what to buy for groceries. How to run the "damn washing machine" nor figure out how to replicate the perfect starching of his collars. He looks at the bills that arrive in the mail with contempt and has all but given up on figuring out his checkbook. He is overwhelmed. So he comes to see me. I go over his billing statement and show him how to read it. Which leads to showing him how to record things into his checkbook and then on to what to buy at the grocery store. I will not allow him to call himself dumb. We talk about all he needs to learn and I give him a few pointers.

Write little notes on his billing statement to help him remember next month and then I get him talking. About everything he knew. His practice, his travels around the world, his wife. I can watch his confidence return and he straightens a little. I know more about complicated heart surgery than ever before and he gets some of his confidence back.

The lesson in all of this became clear after his last visit. As he got ready to leave he asked if he could hug me and left me with this comment - *"I wish I had paid more attention to all areas of my life. I wish that I not only focused on my work, but also on what goes into each day."* His eyes grew wistful and he continued, *"My wife and I had a fairy tale life. Our love and our bond got us through 50 years of marriage, four children and millions of memories. But the one thing I never paid attention to is what it took to have that life. The day – to - day things. Well until now."*

After he left I sat there thinking. How well do you know your own life?

Being part of a marriage or partnership usually means shared responsibilities. Typically one spouse handles the money, the bills etc. and the generally day to day of life. Over time it just gets taken for granted that is how it is done. In my marriage I handle all the finances and the day to day of running our household. It occurred to me after spending so much time with this man that if something should ever happen to me, my husband would be in the same predicament. If something should happen to your spouse or partner tomorrow would you know everything you needed to right away? Like where all of your money is? What your account numbers and insurance polices are? When the next round of bills was due or the interest rate of your mortgage?

Would you be able to run the day to day of your own life?

My guess is after some soul searching and a good honest look, the answer is probably "no" for a lot of people. I know that my husband would be able to feed and clothe himself. But know what bills were due, what bills we even have and how to get to all of our accounts - nope. What about you? The lesson this man taught me is that we all need to know how to run every single facet of our lives. The mundane tasks, like general house repairs, car maintenance, and laundry. As well as the big things; like household finances, accounts and bills. Just because it is something you have never done or had to worry about, doesn't mean you shouldn't learn it. I can't imagine what it would be like at 78 years old, after decades of performing heart surgery, and not be able to balance a checkbook or pay my bills. To not know how to fix a leaky faucet or get my vehicle fixed. These are all things we need to know.

We need to understand and grasp every single facet of our lives. This lesson isn't just for the older crowd either. Life can change for all of us in an instant. Regardless of how old you are or how long you have been together. Spend sometime looking at the day to day of your life. You will be a stronger person for it.

If I Knew Then
What I Know Now

You will face life lessons. You will build your character from the very ground up and you will be in control. Remember your strength, remember your integrity and always remain true to the one person in the world you can always count on- yourself.

Have you ever thought about going back in time and having a conversation with yourself at 18? What would say? What pearls of wisdom would you tell yourself? Would you issue warnings or draw a map of the future? Would you gloss over the bad and focus on the good? What would you say to you?

I thought a bit on this last night. I am coming to a transition period in life, a new chapter if you will. Thus, I have been strolling down memory lane. Mentally strolling along roads that I took to get to where I am today. Crossroads I encountered. Decisions I made. Trials I faced and happiness I experienced. The good, the bad and the ugly. I have had a lot of life lessons in the past 18 years. I am finding at the close of this chapter of my life, I am tired. Mentally tired. But excited at the possibilities. The other morning I was thinking that if there was a way to go back and talk with myself at 18 - maybe I could have avoided some of it. But then I just shook my head when I realized a truth. I would love to sit down with myself back then. But not to give that girl a map to avoid life's pitfalls.

No, I would sit down with her and tell her this:

Nothing lasts forever. People will come in and out of your life. Some will hurt you, some will help you. Some will tear at the very fabric of your soul; while there will be a few to help you heal. You will laugh. You will cry. You will get angry. You will make right and wrong decisions. You will live with the consequences. You will discover in the process of living what you are made of. There will be times of great despair and times of great happiness. You will hit rock bottom and make your way to the top. You will be heartbroken and you will break hearts. You will be broke and you will be flush. Nothing last forever. Happy will fade to sad, sad to angry, angry to understanding. You will face life lessons. You will build your character from the very ground up, and you will be in control. Remember your strength, remember your integrity and always remain true to the one person in the world you can always count on- yourself.

I would look myself directly in the eye and leave her with this:

Never be afraid to see things as they are. Never dull your shine. Take each lesson that life hands to you and learn it. Incorporate it into the fabric of your soul and know that someday, you will use them to help others. Never doubt your place in this world. Just remember it is completely up to you to make it. Be strong. Live first for yourself. Be right with you. Then be there for others. Second guessing yourself gets you no where. Trust your gut, trust your instincts. Never lose your fight. Be strong. You will get to exactly where you need to be.

Trust in that.

We all have things we would have liked to have avoided. But look at it like this. Overspending taught you to budget. The guy you shouldn't have dated, taught you what to look for. Allowing one to control you, taught you the power of your voice when you stood up for yourself. All the bad, all the mistakes, all the life lessons - give you the one thing you weren't born with. **Confidence**. Confidence in yourself and the belief that you can overcome anything. Life teaches you lessons to get you to where you need to be. They hurt. They force you to see and feel things that you really didn't want to. But all of them got you to where you are today. And where you will be tomorrow.

So stop looking at your past as something you wish you could have avoided. Look to it instead for what it taught you. Now take those lessons and put them to use. If you are not happy - do something about it. If someone is taking advantage of you - find your voice and stand up for yourself. Take a life time of mistakes and lessons and own them. They are your story and a powerful one at that.

I am glad that I can't go back. I needed to learn and to grow. To make mistakes and bad decisions. Because as this new chapter of life begins, I am equipped. I know that nothing will break me. That nothing lasts forever. I appreciate what I have, what I have built and what I will do in the future. I understand me. I know that I did the best I could with what I had. Looking back, I wouldn't change a thing.

Haunted

We see ghosts all around us. Only now we call them memories.

When we were young, we convinced ourselves that monsters resided in our closets. That the Bogey Man laid in wait for us under our beds, waiting to feast on our small bodies as soon as the lights went out. We would fight the nighttime with all we had.

Sure that with the coming darkness, the haunting and danger would find us. We hurriedly clamored into bed and pulled our magical blankets around us. We snuggled our trusted stuffed animals to keep us safe and with all of our childish might wished the Bogey Man away. For what seemed like hours we would lay there - willing ourselves awake, the smallest sound to us sounded like claws grabbing at the floor under our beds. We were haunted by imaginary monsters and we weren't afraid of who knew.

Over time we learned tricks that kept the monsters at bay - nightlights to cast away the darkness, our magical blankets that kept us safe from harm and leaving a trail of candy corn that lead to our siblings room as they were far tastier than we were. As we grew older the monsters slowly faded away and for a few short blissful years we were free.

However, the ghosts will find us again in later years. Haunting our minds this time instead of the underside of our beds. The ghosts of regrets and of time gone by. The ghosts of words left unsaid and moments gone forever. We are haunted by loved ones lost, the "could have beens", "should have beens" and "if onlys".

We see ghosts all around us. Only now we call them memories.

The appearance of some ghosts makes us smile and feel warm inside. Driving by that favorite ice cream store that you went to as a child with your grandparents, will bring up the friendly ghosts. Ghosts you don't mind sitting with for awhile. A silvery whisper of the past that crosses your mind leaving a smile at the memory in its wake. But more often than not, the older we get the more haunted our minds become. We trap the memories behind locked doors in the shadowy recesses of our minds. But randomly and usually without warning they break free and float to the forefront of our consciousness. Unbidden. Unwanted. Undeniable. Sometimes frightening and most always bringing the sadness monster in tow. Ghosts of memories of people we will never get back, of moments lost to the sweeping hands of time and the haunting twinge of regret that clogs our throats and sinks into the pit of our stomachs. These ghosts come unbidden, and yet most times are unstoppable. It is almost as if the Bogey Man grew tired of lying around under the beds of children and took up residence in the history section of our minds.

A lesson I have learned recently is this: these ghosts are as much a part of me as the feelings they bring forth. Sometimes our subconscious sees the need to set them free and it is fine to spend some time with them. Even if their presence brings forth sadness, regrets and the overwhelming feeling of loss - they are your ghosts. They are lessons; they are moments in your life that revisiting once in awhile will help you to eventually come to peace with them. Something I know isn't done overnight but eventually can and will happen. Just as when we were younger and chased away the darkness with night lights, the same holds true for the ghosts that haunt us now. We must shine light on them once and awhile. Make peace with them. They are a part of us. If we continually allow them to haunt us and fill our worlds with sadness - we will never truly be happy. We faced the Bogey Man under our beds. We can do the same with the ghosts that haunt our minds.

The key is to not spend so much time among the ghosts of the past that you forget to live today. Some people when you see them wear the monster of sadness draped around their shoulders like a shawl. Their eyes always have that haunted cast and the air around them is heavy. If you wander through the graveyards of times gone by for to long it becomes almost impossible to leave. You are not at peace with the ghosts that haunt you. You just haven't released them long enough to know what life can be like on the other side. Visiting with them once and awhile is fine. It helps release their power over you and eventually find peace. Denying them does you no good either it just increases their power over you and your happiness.

We all have ghosts that haunt us. They serve to remind us that we have loved, we have lived and sometimes there isn't a happy ending. They remind us of times gone by and the lessons we have learned. They are the reminders of what we need to focus on in our present and future. Never take a single thing for granted. Free yourself of regret. Focus on things in your now that you can change. They remind us to be better, do better and to love without fail. They show us that while we can never go back and change the past - we sure as hell can change our future. The ghosts haunt us to help us find peace.

It is up to us to get there.

Unmasked

I am going to let you in on a little secret here -
Some people in this world are not going to like you.
They are not going to accept you nor will they hide it.
If you get through life without making any enemies –
you are doing something wrong.
I know it goes against everything you have
ever been told. But it is true.

Halloween. The time of year when we can put on a costume and become anything we desire - fierce and scary, seductive and sexy, strong and challenging, or angelic and sweet. It is the time of year where we can pretend if even for just for one day to be something we are not.

Or is it?

We tend to wear masks every day of our lives. Our masks only reveal what we want a particular person to see. One version of ourselves to our bosses - another to our children and yet another to our lovers. We will wear a completely different mask when out running errands and still another when visiting family or friends. We mold ourselves fit into the expectations of others. Doesn't that make every day Halloween and the actual holiday - the one day we can show ourselves as we are?

If we continue to go through our lives wearing a multitude of faces and being a multitude of different versions of ourselves; how can we then remember exactly who we really are? This isn't a male/female thing either - we all do it, everyday. What amazes me is that we all do not suffer from multiple personality disorder. We are one person at home and a different version at work. We are moms and dads, and at the same time, husbands and wives. It is like we must splinter ourselves into different shapes in order to be who everyone else needs us to be. How do we meld all of them into one? Is it even possible? How do we even remember who we are exactly?

By allowing ourselves to change into something we are not for someone else, we allow their expectations to dictate who we are in that moment. Often we find ourselves in need of acceptance from them in order to validate who we are or our place in this world. Rarely do we go through an entire day - being exactly as we are. We censor our words, our thoughts and our actions in order to gain approval.

I have a good friend who owns an adult novelty company. By night she is a sexy vixen teaching women about their sexuality. By day she is a mother, a wife and a player in the community. She is involved in every aspect of the lives of her children and their activities. However, because she refuses to mold into an accepted "norm" and behave as a handful of people think she should, she has to defend herself constantly. She volunteers hours and hours of time every week to school and sporting events. But because she refuses to wear a mask to appease others, they scorn her and then try to turn her away. I applaud her.

Because as long as we seek the approval of others and allow them to dictate who we need to be - we will never live true to ourselves. We will continually silence our voice, our thoughts, our very being, in order to gain another's approval. But at what sacrifice?

If we morph ourselves into something less then a true version of ourselves, we run the risk of losing our own unique identity. And in the process, we never give the people in our lives a chance to see us - the real us. Free of all masks, all pretending and variations of our inner truths. The harsh truth of the matter is this; if you are so busy pretending to be something other than the true version of you - the people in your life will continually expect that version. You will eventually lose your essence. Be who you are every minute of every day. Put the masks away and be yourself.

I will let you in on a little secret here - some people in this world are not going to like you. They are not going to accept you nor will they hide it. If you get through life without making any enemies you are doing something wrong. I know it goes against everything you have ever been told - but it is true. Some people are just not going to like you. Shrug your shoulders, brush it off and move along. Because for every one of them, there will be 10 that love you. The real you.

Always be you.

Talking to Myself

I cannot do anything to change the past, but I sure as hell do not have to bring it with me to the future. My future will be as I want it. Sure there will be more life lessons and hard times. But I have kicked ass Before and I can again. I won't let anything break me.

I have conversations with myself all the time. Not out- loud–people–look-at-me- weird - because- I-am-talking-to-myself-conversations; but inside-my-head conversations. Often I am like my own therapist, asking myself questions and then thinking on them awhile before answering - myself. The talking to myself part stems from thinking to much. Often wish I could invent an On/Off switch that could be implanted in my head, as I would love to just shut my damn brain off and relax once in awhile. But until that happens, I am left with my thoughts and my deep philosophical conversations with myself.

My thoughts tend to be like a movie montage. Scrolling along until my subconscious reaches up and plucks one down. Mostly what it pulls down for me to focus on is not what I want to be thinking about, but rather something I need to be thinking about.

Lately, as the first anniversary of my mom's death approaches, a lot of the thoughts plucked down have been about her. I tend to self check myself. Meaning, I gauge how I am mentally on a situation or problem I have been faced with or am currently dealing with. If I can convince myself that I am doing well with something, I can put the thoughts back up on a shelf in my mind and move along. If I am not convinced, I will spend some time reflecting and thinking it through. I tend to be very blunt and upfront with myself. I have to see things as they are. Black and white. I have to face them head on and deal with things as they arise. As I do not want to still be dealing with hard lessons years down the road. I want to face them, deal with them, make peace with them, and then move on.

On a recent *"Random Coffee Talk"* on my Facebook page, I asked my regulars; *"What is the BEST advice YOU have ever given yourself?"* Two things became quickly apparent - I am not alone in talking to myself and I have some pretty insightful fans. As I was reading through all of the pearls of wisdom posted, that subconscious of mine reached up and plucked a thought down for me to look at. All of the wisdom posted on that thread made me realizes we are not at all different from one another. I felt suddenly less alone. As I read the comments I could catch a glimpse of the person behind the advice shared. All had faced life lessons and all had gotten themselves through them.

By spending time talking with ourselves, we are ultimately making peace. Peace within our hearts, our minds, and our souls. We have to pay attention to the thoughts our subconscious randomly brings to our attention. For it is within these thoughts that our greatest fears, sadness and hang ups often live. How much happier and freer could we be if we just let those thoughts flow and talk ourselves through them. Even the unpleasant-make-me-want-to-cry-and-scream thoughts. Let them come to the surface, face them once and for all- then let them go. Don't let the same toxic thoughts repeat themselves over and over, begging for attention. Exam them. Talk yourself through them. We all have the strength inside of ourselves to face and deal with everything life has to hurl at us. We all have those pearls of wisdom floating around inside. We just need to spend sometimes in conversation with our self to hear them.

"To let things go" and *"Always listen to that little voice inside,"* were two bits of advice that resonated strongly with me. That little voice inside my head often whispers to me, let it go. Just let it go. I can not do anything to change the past, but I sure as hell do not have to bring it with me to the future. My future will be as I want it. Sure, there will be more life lessons and hard times. But I have kicked ass before and I can again. I won't let anything break me. As long as I keep talking to myself and facing life head on one thing will always be certain - I got it. Whatever "it" may be. You do to.

Remember that.

Use Your Words

By remaining silent you only hurt yourself. Speak up for what you want,
what you need and what you simply will not tolerate.
Value yourself enough to speak your mind.
Use your words.

I told a good friend of mine today to *"Use Your Big Girl Words."*

She is 43 years old. A mother, a wife, and a professional. She has more inner strength than she gives herself credit for. But what she doesn't have is her voice.

Well she has her voice - just not her inner voice that speaks up for herself. She is getting there slowly. However sometimes she needs that swift kick in the ass to remind her to use her words. Which as her friend I am more than happy to provide. Why? Because she is worth it. Because if she doesn't learn to speak up for herself, for what she wants, what she needs and to set boundaries, people will always walk all over her.

She knows this. But being the gentle soul that she is she doesn't want to hurt anyone. She doesn't want to make demands, say no, or ask for anything. She is in all ways a giver. This is awesome. However, one cannot always give and give and give. Sometimes the givers of this world need to receive.

For many years I silenced my voice. Growing-up what I thought, what I needed and my boundaries did not matter. I learned early on that keeping quiet and just following the party line in my family made life easier. Not better. Not worthwhile. Just easier. Less drama and more peace. I told my mother what she needed to hear in order to make her feel better. I did things that I had no interest in doing because that was what was expected of me. I placated and I went along with her. She was the driving force in my life. I silenced everything in order for her to be happy. I resented it. But it became my normal.

Anyone reading this who knows me is going to chuckle. I am known to be outspoken, blunt and to be relied on to say things that need saying. But what they probably have never realized that until recently - my words were always for others. I never made my voice heard for me. I used my voice for those whose voices were silent for one reason or another. But I never spoke up for myself. Never fought for myself. Until a few years ago when I realized something, if I didn't speak up for what I wanted, deserved or needed - no one was going to do it for me. I had to use my voice and make what I needed and I wanted known. I had to speak up for my happiness, my needs, and I needed to set boundaries. With everyone I cared about and wanted in my life. As well as people I dealt with out in the world.

Using your voice for yourself is not selfish. It is not conceited nor is it bad. Using your voice for yourself gives you power over your own life. You cannot live your life for others before first living for yourself. A lot of people have trouble with this. It feels selfish. Which speaks highly of their character, it is admiral to always want to do for others. But you deserve words too. You deserve to speak your mind and communicate with the world what YOU want. Your needs however basic are important. If you keep sacrificing them for everyone else- what will you be left with?

Think about that for a second. If you never speak up for yourself-never go after what you want, never set boundaries for what is ok for you, what are you left with?

The answer - nothing.

Well... nothing but resentment, lack of confidence and a strong feeling that you are not worth it. This is as far from the truth as you can get. Why is it so hard to say what we feel? Why is it so hard to speak up for ourselves? For some we learned silence at an early age. For others it is a lack of confidence, lack of self worth. But we all need to get over this. You matter. Your thoughts, your dreams and your needs matter. Remind yourself of this.

Use.Your.Words.

Just a Matter of Time

Each moment we have in life is a gift. A gift of time that is guaranteed to no one and more precious than gold. We need to spend more of it on things that matter and less on things that do not.

Time.

Time knows no prejudice. It cares not what color skin you have, what nationality you are nor your social status. You cannot buy time nor can you put some away for a rainy day. The rich and the poor have it in equal amount. One cannot slow it down or speed it up. The seconds tick away to minutes and minutes into hours and the only control you will ever have over it - is what you fill it with.

Back a few years ago when I was sitting with my grandmother in her last few moments of life, I avoided looking at the clock or any thing that reminded me of those precious seconds we had left ticking away. I willed time to slow down with all my might. Over the summer while sitting in the waiting room at the hospital when my husband was having what could be life-altering surgery-,I willed the hands of the clock to go faster. Needing answers, I sat there and wished it would speed up and have the surgery over. Both times I remember hearing the tick-tock of each passing second in my mind. Knowing that regardless of what I did time would continue on - steady. I was reminded of exactly how precious each second of every day is. Every day. Not just those moments in life with so much hanging in the balance.

Time is guaranteed to no one. Each moment we get in life is a gift. Our time on earth could run out at any minute whether we are ready or not. But yet we go through each and every day making promises to ourselves, to our family and friends - when we have more time we will spend it with them. When we have "more time" we will do things that actually matter. Making memories, laughing or just simply sitting with the people we love in silence. We say things like when "time slows down," "when I get more time," or "some time." We are constantly making promises that we don't know if we can keep. We work, we run and we constantly go around in circles never taking a moment to ask ourselves - is it worth it?

We would never run out and spend $1,000 on a purchase without seriously thinking it through. Why then do we squander minutes without a second thought?

People say *"time heals all wounds"* or *"just give it time"* to someone who has experienced something they need to come to peace with. Time does not heal wounds. Time does not make anything better. We do. Time does not make hurt go away. Nor does it heal our internal wounds. All time does is put some distance between the then and the now and leaves the rest up to us. If we spend all of our time hurt, sad, angry and depressed - we will never get it back. As every second you spend looking towards your past is one more second of your now you have lost. The past is just that - past. Those moments are gone and those moments you struggle with- only have power to hurt you if you continue to let it.

As I have grown older, I have come to appreciate time more. That hour in the morning when I first wake up, when the house is silent and I am beholden to no one. That hour of the day is just mine. I treasure it, covet it and understand exactly how important it is. I go to work every day and handle the business of life as all of you do. But what I am slowly realizing is that I need to spend my time like I do my hard-earned money, consciously and with thought. I need to carve time out of my day for the important things. Laughter. Fun. Making memories with the people I love. I need to dedicate time to the things that matter most to me. Writing and creating. Sitting next to the ocean. Snuggled up to my husband just listening to his heart beat. I need to spend my life in the now. Not in yesterday or last year or too much in tomorrow. Right now. Because right now is all I have.

Time seems to fly by so fast. But in truth - time is nothing but steady and consistent. Seconds into minutes, minutes into hours and hours into days. There are never any surprises, no bonus hours in a day. Nothing is guaranteed except that it passes us by whether we want it to or not. Our time is more precious than money- more precious than gold. We need to spend it wisely and enjoy it.

Season of Regenerating

Life cycles much like the seasons. But if we stubbornly cling to things that no longer work for us we will never make room for new growth.

After a rather gloomy stretch of weather, I was greeted with a crisp bright fall morning. Taking my coffee I went out to sit on my porch and breathe in the fall air. My home sits nestled in the Maine woods and I am surrounded by towering trees. There was a slight breeze swaying the tree tops and I found myself staring at my favorite one.

Until a recent rainstorm the leaves on this particular tree had been an array of spectacular fall colors. Rich browns, golds, and yellows that glittered in the sun. However, with the rainy weather and strong winds over the past couple of days, most of the leaves had fallen. They lay strewn across my lawn, blowing here and there in the breeze. I am always sad to see them fall leaving the trees stark and bare.

This morning though as I sat there watching the leaves flutter across my yard- something occurred to me. The barren trees are still very much alive. They have simply pulled into themselves to regenerate - shedding all that was no longer needed. The leaves had served their purpose. Now was the time for the trees to let them go.

Shedding things that no longer serve a purpose in life is as freeing as those trees shedding their leaves. By letting go of all their leaves- they are in essence opening themselves to new growth when the time is right. For them it will be in the spring. But for you and I - it could be tomorrow, next week or like the trees in the spring time.

But let go we must.

We have to strip away all that no longer works in our lives, in our minds and in our souls. All that we hold inside ourselves that may have served a purpose at one time or another but no longer does. Trapped anger that we used as a defense, sadness, self doubt or self recrimination. Bitterness and unhappiness that serves nothing. We have to strip away all the crap that has built up inside of ourselves - right down to our bare essentials. We need to make room to grow.

I reached down and picked up a hand full of leaves. Holding them in my hands I reflected all that I needed to let go. Resentment, hurt, anger and the what-could-have-been and what-should-have been. All of us build things like this up over the years, it is life. But what we never stop to do, really focus on doing is letting it go. Sure being angry will help fuel you through a hard patch and building walls around ourselves to keep the world at bay works for awhile too. But if held onto for too long we only hurt ourselves.

Holding these leaves in my hand, I looked up to the trees. Mostly bare now but on various branches a few stubborn leaves held on for dear life. They did not want to let go. Stubborn - like parts of me. Parts that I had clung to growing up that while at the time may have served a purpose but now longer do. Still I cling to them. Fingering the leaves in my hand I decide now is the time to let it all that no longer serves me or my life-Go. One at a time I let one of the leaves fall and named one thing I knew I no long had room in my life for. Watching as the breeze carried them away I somehow felt free. I knew it would take some work. Old habits are hard to break but by identifying all that I needed to release was a start.

Life cycles much like the seasons. But if we stubbornly cling to things that no longer work for us we will never make room for new growth. It is scary to strip away all that has gotten you this far. All that has sheltered you or protected you. But there must come a time in life when we shed it all. We, like the trees, must draw into ourselves and gather strength from inside our own mind and soul. We need time to regenerate. It doesn't happen overnight, but it will happen. Looking at the trees barren now of their leaves what I see is promise. Promise that in the spring after spending the winter regenerating- they will once again grow anew. Same thing goes for me. I must make room inside my world for only things that will help me grow.

A new season of life.

Someday...

"Someday" doesn't exist, never has, and never will. There is no "someday". There's only today. When tomorrow comes, it will be another today; so will the next day. They all will.
There is never anything but today.

Have you ever counted the times you say the words "someday," during the course of a week? Probably not, as we are all to busy worrying about it, planning for it, working towards it, that we actually forget, it doesn't really exist. Someday I will make enough money to buy her a ring, some day I will take a day off and go on an adventure, some day I will be happy - when I... after I... Someday I will have time. But if some day doesn't exist, that means it never comes. So all the hard work and all the planning is for what? Some day is the ultimate procrastination. All of us are guilty of it, we do it every day and half the time doesn't even realize it. We are so caught up in work and the daily grind that we lose sight of what we have right now. We have today. If you can't see beyond what you think you are working towards, saving for, how will you know when you are there? Rarely do we stop and say. Today is my Some Day. *"Today I am going to make it happen. I am going to tell the person I am with that I love them; I am going to take my kids to get ice cream instead of spending more hours at work. I am going to make my wife put on her fancy clothes (that probably still have the price tags attached) and take her on a date. Today, instead of traveling the never ending road to Someday, I am actually going to arrive."*

The way to get started is to quit talking and begin doing. I mean seriously do we actually think that the world will end if we take the time? Are the planets going to collide and stars fall from the sky? Will our employers have to close the doors because we decided that for one moment in time, we were going to live our someday? Probably not, but we, when faced with this, will fall back on any excuse we can think of as to why it's impossible. What we don't understand is that there is always, "something" and maybe that something can wait til someday to get done.

And it's not just events we put off – it's decisions and changes and life. We stay in situations and hope that someday things will be different, someday she will change, some day he will understand me. Someday I will go after that job, that degree, that guy. Someday I will speak my mind. Someday I will write again *(Yeah that was mine)* and then it's not procrastination, it's plain old fear. Fears of failure, of rejection, and sometimes - fear of success. Because once we get there and we do it, we have no idea what to do next, and that scares us. Thus the cycle continues, and it is a cycle of somedays.

We all need to man up. We all need to take stock of what is important to ourselves, our families, our lovers and friends and stop living on the fantasy island called Someday I'll...

Can you do it?

Rewind-Regenerate-Resolve

As the dawn of the new rear approaches, the time to figure out what to bring with you and what to leave behind - is now.

For as long as I can remember I have always found myself saying goodbye to the current year on December 31, in my own special way. It has varied year to year depending on what I have had to face and what the year was like for me. One year on December 31, I burned an entire box of love letters from a relationship that had ended a few months before. Another year I lit a candle for all of the loved ones I lost and replayed a memory in my mind of them before blowing out the flame. Some years I have written in my journal and other years I have flashed a "Year in Review" montage in my mind. Whatever I have done served one purpose - to say goodbye to the current year. To end the chapter and assess where I wanted to go from there. My way of saying goodbye and putting an end to it with a solid finality.

After my period of review and reflection on what has transpired during the year and time spent with the lessons I learned, trials I faced, my accomplishments and my disappointments - I consciously decide what stays and what goes with me into the new year. I leave behind the hurt and the negative but take the knowledge it gave me. I leave the people who have no place in my future and grab hold of the ones who have loved me, pushed me and accepted me. I do not bring anything into my new year that doesn't serve my growth, my happiness or my life.

Then I bid the year adieu. It was 364 days of my life that I lived, I experienced and now am prepared to move from. I have a fresh new year to fill.

I have never been one for New Year's resolutions. I believe in having goals and dreams throughout the entire year. Just seems logical to start on New Year's Eve with the promise of fresh new start to a fresh new year. It is definitely not a "Do Over" just another chance to get it right or even better- get me right. A new year is not just a date on the calendar, but a moment in your life when at midnight on December 31, you have your first moments of perfection. A moment without any mistakes, any disappointments, loss or sadness, a pristine new year. Don't get me wrong here - I am totally a realist and I know that the normal bullshit will eventually filter through - it is life after all. But if you spend some time saying your goodbyes to the current year and then decide what will make it into your new year - you will totally be ready, clean and mistake free for at least the first few minutes of January 1st.

One year at about 11:30 pm I went outside on my deck and stared up at the night sky and millions of twinkling stars filled my vision. There was so much that year I needed to make peace with. A year that had spun completely out of control and all I could do was hang on for the ride. A year of loss, of confrontation and resignation. I still had so much anger and frustration come the last day of the year, saying goodbye to it was one of the hardest yet. Looking up at the night sky I replayed it in my head - all of it. I knew that I couldn't allow any of the bad to go forward with me. Silently I closed the chapter. None of those feelings had a place in my new year. I had to let them go to stay right where they were - in the past.

Looking up to that night sky I said goodbye and welcomed the new year and at the very stroke of midnight a shooting star shot across the sky. For my first moment in the new year I made my wish and felt something I hadn't felt in a long time - hope.

As the dawn of the New Year approaches the time to figure out what to bring with you and what to leave behind - is now.

Shades of Gray

Not everything in life is black and white. Not everything is clear cut and clean. Life is messy. Feelings and emotions are messy. But it is within the shades of gray that we can reach out to others and find that middle ground. For it is within the shades of gray that peace resides . Where you are honored for your beliefs and truths and so am I.

We do not see things as they are. We see things as we are. Our truths and perspectives on situations in life may be right for us, may feel right for us, but in truth, they are simply our personal spin on it.

Just because I look at the night sky and see the stars do not mean that you will look and see the same thing. You could look up at the same night sky and only see emptiness and black. When I look at a person with multiple piercings and purple hair - I see is someone expressing his or her individuality. What someone else sees could be completely different. Neither of us would know the truth - the real truth. What we see is only our perception of the truth. We don't see who that person actually is, only what they appear to us to be. So snap are our judgments we rarely take the time to find out.

Life is not always black and white.

What is right for one will not always be right for another. We tend to see the world as we are - our past, our upbringing, our beliefs and our experiences shape how we view life and everything in it. How we judge people, events and everything we hold to be "truth" rest solely on our very personal views. But in reality, truth is relative.

There is no universal truth - a-one-size-fits-all to any situation in life we are faced with.

You look at a situation one way and I look at it another - neither of us is wrong in our minds. We judge situations and events on how we react to them. We often do not stop long enough to see things from any other perspective. Rarely do we stop ourselves and study the shades of gray that permeate our existence every day. Why would we, when we are so convinced that we are right?

Life is a series of shades of gray.

People make assumptions. People make even more assumptions in the heat of the moment. Assumptions fueled by anger, sadness and moral indignation are so black and white it leaves no room for discussion. No room for communication. It is you vs. them or me vs. you and seriously it doesn't have to be this way. What really gets to me is when people make assumptions about my life, my actions and never ask me directly why I handled things a certain way, or reacted to something a certain way. People only see what they want to see and that is it. Black and white.

When we do not honor another's view, feeling or belief, we are in essence forcing ours on them. We will argue and stand our ground for we feel we are right. And we are - for ourselves. But we can never know without a doubt- what is truth and what is right for anyone other than ourselves. There is no way to know the truth of another based solely on our perceptions. We must talk, we must ask questions and we must be open to the fact that we may never agree and that is ok. We don't have to. What we need to do is respect that fact and move on. Life is too short to be arguing.

In fact, if we spent less time arguing who is right and who is wrong and spending more time on developing the shades of gray into compromise think of all we could accomplish. How much hurt would be soothed in families? How many friendships would be saved? Go even further - How many tragic events in life could have been avoided if we spent more time coming together with our differences instead of splitting apart at the seams because of them.

Be open to the shades of gray in life.

Understand that just because you believe your version or explanation of events to be true - what you see and how you feel may not necessarily be the absolute truth for someone else. Respecting this concept could stop so much wrong in the world. Honoring one-another- be it family members, strangers on the street, anyone who looks out and sees a different view then you - would be amazing. We must let go of the ego. We must let go of the need to be right for everyone but ourselves. We must let go of the blame and the anger and allow others the room to be right as well. We will not be sacrificing what we believe or what we hold to be true as it is still right for us. But we must allow others to be right for themselves as well.

Not everything in life is black and white. Not everything is clear cut and clean. Life is messy. Feelings and emotions are messy. But, it is within the shades of gray that we can reach out to others and find that middle ground. For it is within the shades of gray that peace resides. Where you are honored for your beliefs and truths and so am I. Where black and white combine together and go forward.

Casting Stones: Finding Lessons

There will always be good in this world. There will always be bad. It is life. It is a balance. And when something happens to disrupt that balance it is up to us to do something to correct it. You cannot go back and erase what has happened, but you can go forward, learn from it, and then, cause ripples of your own.

I am standing on the shore of a nearby lake. It's early morning; the sun is just rising over the treetops. There is no wind and no noise. It is perfect stillness. The lake is like a silver mirror. When I look out at this smooth flawless body of water I am reminded of peace. How every day begins like this. Calm. Serene. That first moment when you open your eyes from sleep.

Those precious few moments when you blink the slumber from your eyes and have yet to have a thought. For that brief moment everything is in perfect balance. Standing at the shore I pick up a pebble and softly lob it into the water.

Immediately circles ripple out from where it hits and sinks. Ripple after ripple. I bend to pick up a larger stone. Using more strength I throw the stone into the once again calm water. It hits with a splash! Bigger ripples circle out and out. Again I bend to pick up another stone. This one by far bigger. I heave it with all my might into the mirrored surface of the lake. Splash! Ripple after ripple as far as I can see radiate outwards.

It is in this moment when I realize, from the smallest pebble to the biggest stone, each broke the calm and sent ripples out into the lake. Like the smallest action can send ripples into the world, everything we do has consequence. Everything we do, everything we say, everything we feel sends ripples out. To our family, to our friends and coworkers. To strangers that do not even know our name.

Do you believe that there is good in this world? I do. I also know that if I am to believe there is good, I must also believe there is bad. I have seen both. I have experienced both. I know that this is true. I know each causes ripples when it occurs. I have seen one good deed lead to another.

I have seen what one person can do when reaching out, helping or just listening to some one in need. Then seeing that person go on and reach out to others. So on and so forth. Ripples of good spreading out into the world. Each starting with one. I have also seen the other side of life. How one evil act can affect not only the one it was directed at but also cast out and touch others as well. I have seen evil that not only destroy the victim, but the victim's families, friends, and communities, as well. One act of evil seems to infinitely reach out into the world.

Perpetuating good deeds and good actions are easy. But standing up in the face of bad, in the face of evil, and breaking the rippled circle as it spirals out is so much harder. When I was at the lake, directly after I threw the biggest stone, I noticed that at about 20 rippled circles out from the center, close to the shore, there was a branch sticking straight up out of the water. It broke the ripple by standing firm. But having its roots in the ground. It forced a break. So it is in life, when evil happens. When something so awful so horrific happens that the effects of it are felt across the community, the state and the nation. We must break that ripple of fear. We must break it and respond with love and support. But most of all- with strength.

On December 14, 2012 a horrific act of evil happened in Newtown, Connecticut. A lone man planned and plotted an attack on innocents. The effect was immediate and far reaching. Rallying calls that schools are no longer safe were on every news station. The desperate need to place blame on someone and to know – why did this happen, overwhelmed the nation. The ensuing panic that erupted and the ripples out from Newtown were swift, they were harsh and they incited fear. One man's evil act was the catalyst that caused this. There will never be the "one answer" that explains it all. Motive or no, it happened. Now we must all be like that branch in the water. We must stand firm. We must brace ourselves and break the ripple of fear. One man acting alone does not make every school unsafe. We must break the ripple and we must create one of our own. The smallest gesture can sometimes have the biggest effect.

Do something.

I created a small picture with a candle on that Friday afternoon. It simply said "Prayers for for the children, staff and families at the Sandy Hook Elementary School." I live in Maine hundreds of miles away. But I needed to do something for those people. I put it up on my Random Thoughts fan page on Facebook. The candle has been shared more than

300,000 times. When I look at the lists of people who shared it, a lot had also included a message that rippled out to their friends; their friends shared it and added their own. So forth and so on. One little gesture sent all those thoughts out to the world. I was stunned. What that one little candle did was break that evil ripple. Broke it and in turn sent positive healing ripples out of its own.

Do not let the evil of one man's actions ripple out. Do not let it cause you to question your beliefs, your Gods or the good in this world. Do not let it cause fear. Break that ripple. Stand firm. Do something good, something random no matter how small. That act alone will cause a break. That random act will spur on another and another sending good ripples into the world.

There will always be good in this world. There will always be bad. It is life. It is a balance. And when something happens to disrupt that balance it is up to us to do something to correct it. You cannot go back and erase what has happened, but you can go forward, learn from it and cause ripples of your own.

Everything Happens for a Reason. Right?

Everything in life does in fact NOT happen for a reason and there is not always a lesson to be learned. Sometimes bad things happen to good people. Sometimes life will just not make sense.

The other day I was having a conversation with a friend who is trying to make sense out of something that happened to her a long time ago. She is struggling with putting a rational spin on it in order to come to some form of peace inside herself. Seeing her struggle and twist and turn things over in her mind to no avail was heart wrenching.

Life can deal some nasty blows to us. We wake up one day and start off thinking good positive thoughts and having a great morning when all of a sudden out of the blue, a phone call, a knock at the door, changes our entire existence. Just like that, our world can be turned upside down and we are left with broken pieces of something that not long ago was whole. We are left lost, confused and shattered. After the initial shock wears off we find ourselves in desperate need to make sense of what has occurred. The "Why" of it. We know what happened, we know that we need to face it and deal with it. But what we don't know is the how. How do you deal with the bad? How do you find your peace? How do you put it behind you and move on?

Everyone always tells you that you need to just get passed "it." You need to make peace with "it." That you need to just let "it" go. But what no one tells you is how to do this. How do you just let it go? Does not thinking about it work? Does therapy work? Does anger work? They tell you to cry and to talk it out. But talking just makes it real and crying, while cleansing, solves nothing. We try to make rational sense out of an event that wasn't rational to begin with. We look for that elusive "reason" everyone says things happen for and make ourselves crazy in the process.

How do you find that reason and that lesson everyone always says things happen for?

You don't.

Sometimes a life event will happen that defies reason. That no amount of examining will help you explain. Some things in life will never make sense because there is NO sense to be had. No cause and effect, no lessons that needed to be learned and there sure as hell will never be a rational reason behind it. It just happened. There is no making sense of it. You face it. You look it square in the eye and remove all the shields and walls you have put up and you face it once and for all. You don't get past it until you confront it and see it for what it is. Then you leave it there.

You can't erase the bad; you can't erase the tragic any more than you can make sense of it. It happened. It became part of you the second that it happened and denying its existence, not seeing it for what it is, will never change that. Visiting it inside your mind over and over will not change the fact that it happened. It will not change the outcome or make it any less painful. But understanding that some things in life will never make sense gives you the power over it, instead of it having power over you.

Sometimes bad happens. Out of the blue and without warning. The whole *"everything happens for a reason"* phrase is ridiculous. I could spend my whole life searching for reason behind losing my friend to a drunk driver or why the child on the news last night was beaten by his parents and left for dead. I could search high and low for the lesson to be learned in the why bad things happen to good people and the reason behind every life event I have had to face. But there are times in life when you are never going to be able to make rational sense out of a life even because there is none.

When I realized the futility of always trying to find "the why" - of trying to make sense out of the senseless, the release I had was astounding. I didn't have to hold on to the hurt anymore. I could let it go. My peace was only elusive because I was holding it at bay while I tried everything I could to find a reason for what happened.

Just like my friend who was struggling with her own life event - she couldn't see her way passed it until she realized that the why of it didn't matter. It happened. She didn't deserve it. Nothing she had done in her life warranted this particular lesson. It just happened. Once she realized that no amount of soul searching was going to give her the "reason" or make sense of it, she allowed herself to let go of it.

She found her peace by not making sense of a senseless life event.

Everything in life does in fact NOT happen for a reason. Sometimes shit happens. You can spend your whole life twisting and turning it over and over in your head. You can spend countless nights staring at the ceiling and countless days lost in it. But the sooner you realize making sense out of a senseless event is impossible, the sooner you will be able to come to peace with it and move on with your life.

Your Life:
Your Responsibility

Take responsibility for your life and stop finding excuses, scapegoats and reasons why something wrong isn't your fault. Your life and your decisions are yours - own them.

It is Monday morning. You forgot to set your alarm the night before and you wake up late. You rush through a shower, grab some coffee and fly out the door. You cannot be late to work again. Off you go breaking one traffic law after another. Stop signs, red lights and speed limits mean nothing to you as you try and make it to work on time. You hit an open stretch of highway and hit the gas - nothing in your way now.

Suddenly out of nowhere, blue lights in the review mirror. Busted. Litanies of plausible excuses immediately run through your mind as the trooper ambles up to your window. When he asks as they all do - *"do you know why I pulled you over?"* You decide on coy and plead ignorance. When he tells you that you were 17 miles over the limit, you "breakdown" and blame everyone but the one person who deserves it. Yourself. Hearing it all before the trooper writes you a ticket. In your mind you vow to fight it. You end up late to work and furious at the cop for making you late.

Personal Responsibility - our own cause and effect.

Our actions determine our life. Our actions determine our happiness, our success and our failures. Yet when we make a mistake we spend more time finding other people to blame and creating excuses as to why something isn't our fault, than we do fixing it and making it better so that we can move on.

I was having a conversation the other day with a friend. He is always late. His excuse is that tardiness runs in his family, he can't help it. Really? I have another friend who has a daughter in her early 20s who has made some really poor life decisions as of late. What 20 year old doesn't? But to hear her mother talk none of it is her daughter's fault. *"She takes after her father - he is so lazy."* Or my personal favorite - *"she keeps losing her jobs because she is just like me and can't focus on boring things like answering phones."* I looked at my friend and asked her if she thought making excuses for her daughter was helping her in the long run. What was she teaching her? She made me shake my head when she said, *"Moms are supposed to cover for their children."*

No, parents are supposed to teach their children to be responsible for their actions. Teach them to make good decisions and how to learn from their mistakes. Teach them cause and effect. Teach them that their decisions directly affect their life.

We all make mistakes. We get into relationships that are not healthy. We break speed limits. We cheat on diets and we run late. We break our own rules and we sometimes make bad decisions. It is called life. The problem is most will blame everyone else for what happens to them. How is it that we think we control our lives if we say we have no control over even the simplest actions like being on time? If you are constantly cheating on your diet because a coworker brings in treats, it is not the coworker's fault. It is yours. If you are constantly late, it is not the traffic or your alarm clock - it is you. If you are constantly dating men or women who break your heart, cheat on you or worse, that is on you too. You have 100% control of only one thing in this life. Yourself.

Your health, your time management, your happiness and your life is no one's responsibility but your own. Own your mistakes. Stop blaming bad habits on family traits. Break the cycle. If everyone in your family has the same problem - be the one who owns it and DOES something about it. Stop letting it go just because everyone else has.

Take responsibility for your life and stop finding excuses, scapegoats and reasons why something wrong isn't your fault. If you need help - ask for it. If you need to learn how - research it. If you need to stop making the same mistakes over and over again - look for the reasons behind why you do what you do. If you stop blaming outside forces for your own mistakes, you will find solutions so much faster.

Stop the *"It is not my fault because..."* and instead try the *"Yes I screwed up, now what am I going to do about it..."* Take Responsibility for the only thing in this life you can control - **YOU!**

Duct Tape and Tin Foil

*It's amazing what you can accomplish with a little
Imagination and a dozen rolls of duct tape.*

It sat there - the final gift under the Christmas tree. A huge box wrapped in shiny green paper that came up to my hip and much to my excitement had my name on it. As I reached down to pick it up I was stunned at the heaviness of it. Reading the tag I saw that it was a gift from my grandmother. I remember looking over to her and seeing her smirk. She looked pretty proud of herself. Getting excited, I plopped right down on the floor and got ready to open it.

The Old Bat *(that's what we affectionately called her)* told me to wait. She had something to say. She got up from the couch and walked over to me. Putting her hand on my shoulder she looked down at me *"Remember that anything in life that is important - you have to work for"* she said. *"Sometimes the things you have to really put an effort into reap the most reward."* I remember ribbing her a little about being so deep on Christmas morning. Looking me square in the eye she chuckled and patted me on the head.

Once she was back on the couch and had her camera ready I reached for the present. Shocked again at how heavy it was, I pulled at the tape on the side and grabbed a chunk of paper. With a dramatic flourish I tore off the shiny paper! What the hell was this? I remember thinking to myself, as I pulled off the remaining paper.

The entire box was covered in miles and miles of Duct Tape.

Twelve rolls to be exact. With no end in sight to pull on, I was temporarily flummoxed. What the hell? Who wraps a present in duct tape? Her childish laughter gave me my answer, she did. She stood up and proclaimed that I was going to be a while and she needed a smoke, chuckling as she walked away. For the next 45 minutes I pulled, tore and swore as I made my way into this present. Finally I made it to cardboard. The end was in sight! Pulling the flaps of the box I look inside. Five cans of peas, a bunch of large rocks, a fire starter log and about a whole role of paper towels... What the hell? I started removing it all and discover another box! This one not only wrapped in duct tape but tin foil too! Tin

Foil and Duct Tape!?! The smaller box was slightly easier to get into. As I pulled the flaps open I found… three cans of carrots, two cans of corn and one can of chicken soup. Seriously? At the very bottom of the box was a small white jewelry box.

My heart stopped. Immediately I knew what it was. Tears sprang to my eyes as I pulled it out and opened it. Nestled inside of the box was my great grandmother's watch. A watch she had worn for years and had passed on to my grandmother. This watch was not worth a lot of money, nor was it particularly fashionable but it represented the two most important women in my life.

I sighed as I looked around the living room at the mountains of duct tape, tin foil, canned vegetables, rocks and paper towels. The watch weighed all of four ounces and fit into a box about three inches long and two inches deep. My grandmother looked very proud of herself.

A tradition was born.

From that Christmas forward, no one was safe. There would always be at least one present wrapped in rolls and rolls of duct tape and a half a roll of tin foil.

Two stand out in my mind the most.

One year my sister bought her husband a 42" flat screen TV. She, my grandmother and my 7-year old step son spent four hours wrapping it in duct tape, the Sunday comics and tin foil. Eight rolls of duct tape went onto that one and took him almost an hour and a half to get into it. Another time was a few years back; I had found a one-of-a-kind autographed baseball for my husband. This ball had been a treasured keepsake of one of the Groundskeepers at Fenway Park in Boston. He had over a span of 30 years, gotten, more than 25 autographs of his favorite Red Sox players. Starting in the 1920s and going to the 1950s. Big names in baseball like - Williams and Yastrzemski to name a couple. Took me more than two hours and four boxes, four cans of spaghetti sauce, a couple of rocks, four rolls of duct tape, one roll of tin foil and two rolls of Christmas wrapping paper to get it done.

Every time I get excited about a gift I have found for a loved one my grandmother's words echo in my ears—*"Remember that anything in life that is important - you have to work for."* She's gone now but her memory is as strong as the duct tape and as shiny as the tin foil I wrap around these presents. Sometimes I swear I can hear her chuckle.

Sticks and Stones

One of the hardest lessons in life is knowing when to walk away. To cut the ties that bind us to people we love. But love should never hurt. Love should never leave you feeling empty and alone and worthless. Value yourself enough to know this and know that you can walk away.
You can silence the voices and move on.

Hurtful words will echo in your mind long after the voice that speaks them is silent. As a record with a scratch repeating the words over and over, so do the words that cut us greater than any knife could. Even if the words are spoken in anger or as an off-the-cuff remark, you feel them. You hear them and you worry them over in your mind until there comes a point that you start to believe them. If they came from someone you love, you respect and you cherish, well more often than not you incorporate them into your very being. As the ones who love us never wish to hurt us, right? But what if in the moment these words were spoken that is the very thing they wanted most?

Sometimes the people we love will say or doing something that hurts our feelings. That breaks our hearts and makes us second guess everything we believe about ourselves, for it is only those closest to us who hold that power. They hold that power, though, not by simply being family, spouse or friend. They hold that power because we give it to them.

We give it to them with the belief that they will always use it to build us up when we stumble, build our confidence when it shakes and to always reaffirm that we are in fact loved and cherished. And sometimes that is exactly what they do. But sometimes the one we love will take that power so freely entrusted to them and use it not to build you up but instead use it to bring you down.

A childhood friend of mine had a father who would constantly berate her, tell her she was worthless and would amount to nothing. That she was fat and ugly and no man would ever want her. She strove for excellence in everything she did to prove her worth. She won awards, she got amazing grades and she was a warm and caring person. She was a daughter to be proud of. Except he never was. And over the years his hurtful words and actions broke her. She stopped caring. She believed everything he ever told her. Things no parent should ever say to a child. She carried his words all through her life. She formed friendships but always kept them at arm's length. She rarely dated and felt completely unworthy of attention. She was never good enough she believed, because her father had said so. Until one day she decided to take her power back.

She took away his power to hurt her by simply walking away from him.

One of the hardest things in life is to know when it is time to walk away. We all have different thresholds to what we will tolerate from those closest to us. Family, spouses or friends are a part of our lives because we want them there.

But, what do you do when someone you care about hurts you over and over again? How many chances do you give someone until you throw your hands up and say no more? Personally, I have mastered the art of walking away. Part of me is proud of the fact that I will not tolerate being hurt repeatedly, lied to or disrespected over and over by anyone. Another part of me wonders if maybe I walk away too easily. It is the age old battle of mind versus heart in these matters and it is a battle all of us face at one time or another.

When is enough - enough?

I am all for second chances in most cases. We all make mistakes. But if someone you care about hurts you over and over again chances are it is not by mistake. Like the saying goes, *"Fool me once shame on you. Fool me twice shame on me."* We shouldn't continually sacrifice ourselves for anybody, yet we do. Over and over again. We tolerate being hurt by the very people that should never hurt us. Parents, spouses, family members or friends should not get a pass just because of who they are.

Words have the power to hurt you only as long as you allow it. I don't care if you share DNA with the one who spoke them or not. You do not need anyone to validate you except for the one person who knows you better than anyone - yourself. Take your power back from those that use it to hurt you and use it instead to fuel you on. Never let anyone make you second guess something you know in your heart is true.

Trust and Value Yourself.

One of the hardest lessons in life is knowing when to walk away. To cut the ties that bind us to people we love. But love should never hurt. Love should never leave you feeling empty and alone and worthless. Value yourself enough to know this and know that you can walk away. You can silence the voices and move on.

You are worth it.

Standing on the Sidelines

It is one of the hardest things in life we face.
Our powerlessness to help someone we love.

I remember sitting there in the brightly lit emergency room blind to the hustle all around me. The stringent smell of antiseptic in my nose and the nervous feeling in my belly. I had grown accustomed to the wait and the fear as I had been in this ER so many times at that point with my husband that it was starting to feel like home. Each time with the same goal in mind - getting my husband to breathe normally.

I sat and watched him struggle for the very air so many of us took for granted. Knowing that there was absolutely nothing I could do for him to make it better. Except love him and keep my shit together.

It was during one of the many visits to the ER that I had a huge life epiphany that would carry across to many situations I would face in my life. As I sat there with him holding his hand I realized my breathing had changed. I was taking deep lung fulls of air and calmly releasing them. Over and over.

I had been trying to breathe for him.

I did not even realize I was doing it. So great my need to help him - I wanted to breathe for him. It was crushing at the time to come to the conclusion that regardless of how hard I tried, how strong I willed it and how much power I could put behind it, I would never be able to breathe for him. The powerlessness and guilt were overwhelming.

It was a life lesson that I will never forget.

It is one of the hardest things in life we face. Our powerlessness to help someone we love. To grab the reins and step in to make it all better. Sometimes we can't breathe for them. Sometimes they have got to be the one to breathe on their own. Regardless of how much love we have for them. How much strength we have to give them. How much insight and ideas we have to help them make a better life, better choices or get to a better place. Sometimes we can't. Sometimes we have to step back.

Sometimes a loved one is facing or dealing with something that regardless of how hard we try, how hard we pray; only they can fix. While we remain on the sidelines cheering them on, offering support or a safety net. Just so they know they are not alone.

I had a friend once who was in an abusive relationship. I knew it. She knew that I knew it. I tried thousands of times to get her to leave him. I loved her, I got angry for her and I offered a place to stay. She never left him. All I could do was stand by and watch her struggle. I was powerless to do anything but be her friend. I couldn't help her until she realized she was ready. I couldn't breathe for her.

Sometimes life gives you situations that you will never be able to control. That you will always remain a bystander and it is one of the hardest roles to become accustomed to. A son or daughter fighting addiction. A relative with a mental illness or a friend in an abusive relationship.

Sometimes we will be faced with something that we can't fix. The push to try harder and to never give up motivating us to the point of exhaustion. To give as much love and guidance as we can. The guilt eats away at our soul and we are left standing there no further ahead. While we watch our loved one struggle, fight or just give up. We can no more walk their path for them, make better decisions for them or get them to want our help, than I could breathe for my husband in the ER.

Sometimes we can't save the very people we love. And, it is important to know that it is not your fault. That while you did everything in your power to help them. Loved them beyond measure and would have walked across fire for them. You couldn't walk their path. You couldn't live their life for them and while hard to swallow and devastating - you couldn't change the outcome. The stark and honest truth here is - only they could. It was never your place to make the changes they so desperately needed. Nor could you have done any more than you did. They walked the path of their life. You walked along side them. You supported and loved them. You gave them everything they needed.

Sometimes there are happy endings. But sometimes there are not. Sometimes life had different outcomes in mind that we never saw coming. The guilt and the-could-have-beens eat away at our soul. The *"If only I had tried harder"* or *"Loved them more."* **Stop.** You know inside of your very soul that you gave all you had and then some. If they are still making bad life decisions all you can do know is love them. Be there to catch them should they fall.

Always know that it is their path to walk, and while you can walk beside them, you can never walk for them. For as it is our destiny to walk our own life path, it is also their destiny to walk their own path as well.

Letting Go of Letting Go

*I am tired of letting things go. By letting them go and swallowing my
words because it is easier than calling someone I care about out on how
their behavior hurts me, angers me or that I feel disrespects me -
I am in essence giving them permission to continue.*

On my drive home there is a stretch of road that is two lanes for a mile or
so. At the end of this stretch, the driving lane continues on straight and
the left lane is to turn left. It never fails that the lane to go straight backs
up at the time I am heading home from work. It also never fails that at
least two cars will shoot past the line of traffic and force their way in.
The drivers who jump the line and force their way into traffic see only
their needs, wants and are in their own little world. They carelessly
disregard every one waiting.

I have narrowly avoided daily collisions because someone felt that they
could force their needs on me and I either need to swerve out of their
way or risk getting run over. I get irritated every time it happens. Not
because I may have to sit through another light, but because someone is
forcing their will, their decisions and their behavior on me and I have to
accept it or risk an accident.

Not OK on this stretch of road. Also not acceptable in life.

Family members, friends, coworkers, even neighbors force their needs,
their wants and their actions on you. If it is something you do not agree
with, validate or condone, you are still forced to simply accept them,
challenge them or just let it go.

Accepting them is of course the easiest route to take. But what if you
don't? What if what they are doing, saying or not doing goes against your
need or want? What if what they are doing is something you have asked
them not to? When their actions directly affect you and yet you are either
not consulted on the matter or if you are and you disagree they just go
ahead with what they wanted all along? Do you challenge them or just let
it go?

I think most of us time and time again take the easy road and just let it
go. We get labeled if we challenge too much as mouthy, difficult, bitchy

or just plan unaccommodating. But if it is something that happens over and over again and you get disregarded for another's wants or actions, when do you put your foot down and say no more?

Probably when you snap.

I don't what has gotten into me lately. I think that I have hit my limit of just letting stuff go. Gasp! Did I just say that? What will people think? I may get called difficult. I may even get called bitchy. But oddly enough at this point in time, I am OK with that.

What changed? No idea. Well that is not completely the truth. I have some idea. I am tired of letting things go. By letting them go and swallowing my words because it is easier than calling someone I care about out on how their behavior hurts me, angers me or makes me feel disrespected - I am in essence giving them permission to continue.

Well that and the fact I'm just over it.

Growing up with a severely bi-polar mother, I perfected the art of placating. Of shelving what I wanted, needed or felt in order to keep the peace. Always trying to avoid the ultimate fight that would ensue if I actually stood my ground about something that mattered to me. It was easier to just let it go. I find now that I am done always placating everyone else. Sometimes it is appropriate, of course. I don't need to always get my way or what I may want. But when it comes to something I feel strongly about, or if it is something a person does over and over again even after I speak my mind - I just walk away. Completely.

The only people who deserve a place in your life are the ones who hear you, who respect you and the ones who don't force you to either swerve out of their way or risk a collision. It simply isn't worth it. I hit my limit it appears slowly over the past couple of months. If I speak up about something I feel strongly about and I am consistently disregarded by anyone, well then they do not deserve a place in my life.

I am letting go of letting go. If that makes me a difficult, opinionated and mouthy, well then I guess that just means I am doing something right. I am doing something right for me.

You should too.

The Breaking Point - Is Now

We are all flawed creature, and in that, share a common bond with the
rest of the world. You are no less awesome for your flaws than I am. I am
just the type of person who embraces them. I cherish my flaws because
without them I would not have a measuring
stick to see all the good in me.

When will you be good enough...for you? Is there some magical breaking point when one throws their hands up and just accepts everything about them as is? Why is this so hard? I asked this question recently on the Random Thoughts Facebook page. The prevailing answer I read over and over again: I'm learning to. You learn to like coffee, you learn how to drive, and you learn how to eat a lobster. What you shouldn't have to do is learn to love and accept yourself.

With the new year in full swing all I keep hearing about is resolutions. *"I'm going to the gym." "I'm going to lose weight." "I am going to stop being such a pushover." "I'm going to save more money."* It is all about people resolving to change themselves. Don't get me wrong - getting healthy and saving money is awesome. Standing up for yourself is key in life. These are all attainable goals to better yourself.

However, you should **BE** yourself in the process.

If the next line was to say *"name 25 things you would change about yourself"* many of us would start flicking out fingers as we named the list. But if I said *"name 25 things you **wouldn't** change about yourself for anything,"* most would get stumped after five. Even five would be hard for a lot of us. It would be a struggle to say it out loud let alone list 25 things we wouldn't change for anything. But ask us what we would change and we are off. Changing and growing are incredibly important in life. But, isn't being comfortable in your own skin as is, super important too? You are you and no one else in this world can take that away from you - as long as you don't let them.

Once upon a time, I really cared how the world viewed me. I think we all have at one time or another. Especially through the school years when it was natural to compare yourself to others and common to be judged by everyone around you. It is a rite of passage, and one that is so incredibly painful to go through. But it teaches us the lesson that we are different. That we are not cookie-cutter molds of the same person replicated over and over again. That we are who we are and that is OK. Some people aren't going to like you and yet others will cherish the ground you walk on. But neither matter if you do not cherish yourself. So quick we are to write ourselves off as not being good enough, strong enough or handsome enough. We base our total worth on scales, on bank accounts and on everyone else's opinion of something only we truly can know.

Ourselves.

We feel shame because of circumstance. We make mistakes, we stumble and we make really awful decisions. We are all flawed creatures, and in that, share a common bond with the rest of the world. You are no less awesome for your flaws than I am. I am just the type of person who embraces them. I cherish my flaws because without them I would not have a measuring stick to see all the good in me.

My flaws prompt me to be a better person and serve to motivate me to find ways that I can improve myself. What I won't allow is my flaws to stop me or define who I am. I don't care how old you are, if you are single, married or divorced. I don't care if you swear like a sailor or stress-eat. These are just circumstances. These things are life's trappings. These things do NOT define you.

Circumstances you may need to accept. Circumstances may need to be changed or learned how to handle in life. But you are not a circumstance. You are you. You are not your past, you are not your future and you sure as hell aren't here by accident. You have a reason to be here and that is what you must learn. But you must accept yourself - flaws and all. You must. Because right now - this very moment YOU are perfect. Just as you sit there and read this. This exact moment in time finds you completely acceptable. You are not defined by the clothes you are wearing. You are not defined by size. You are not defined by illness. You are defined by simply being.

It is hard to drown out the voices that make us doubt ourselves. The voices that bring us down and hold us there. People who we care about tend to hurt us the most. We come to believe all the negative they say and the limits they place on us. We allow their judgments to define our lives and to dictate our worthiness. It hurts because we believe them. The ones who love us aren't supposed to lie, so what they say about you must be true. Wrong. Wrong. Wrong. Who you are is not defined by anyone outside of you. What they think about you, about your life or your circumstances - are none of your business. Live your life as you are and if they can't accept that, well then walk away. It is not your responsibility to make anyone in this world accept you. They either do or they don't. Such is life and the ones who don't - Well you just don't need them.

That magical moment where you suddenly accept yourself as is...is right this very moment. Now.

Not when you, after you or when you can.

Now.

From the Author

Throughout my life I have been blessed with Earth Angels. Strangers that became lifelong friends and who have touched my soul. They helped make me who I am today. By encouraging me, challenging me and calling me out when needed. I will forever be grateful for them walking into my world and never leaving.

I would like to say thank you to some of these amazing souls.

Marc & Trey: *There are no words to tell you both how much I love you. I love you all the way to the moon AND back to the dirt. You both are my foundation and the family I always dreamed of.* ♥

Aaron Smith: *The freckled face kid that walked into my life and never left. Forever side by side. Love ya bro.* ♥

Laura Smith: *I asked for a sister for Christmas and I got you. Best present ever. Proud of everything you have become. It has been a rough road getting here, but nothing but the best going forward.* ♥

Jane O. Torres: *Thank you Queenie for being like a mother to me. For always listening, being there and loving me like your own.* ♥

Richard Szczepanowski: *My Richie. Without you and your patient editing and consulting – none of this would have been possible. Thank you for helping me not sound like a bumbling idiot.* ♥

Sheila Burke: *My soul sistah. Thank you for helping me see what I was capable of. Of helping me realize my dreams. Thank you for always being my most treasured sounding board. <4 Always.* ♥

Elaine Landry: *Throughout my entire life you have remained one of the few people that I could always believe in, trust and rely on. You will forever be an earth angel to me and I am so grateful to have you in my life.* ♥

About the Author

Who is J.V. Manning?

She is at times her own best friend and at times her own worst enemy. Somedays she has her stuff together. Somedays she is a hot mess. She drinks way too much coffee, but always seems to be tired. She thinks a lot – probably too much. Her brain never really shuts off. She is quirky. She is a bit random. She is a tad bit crazy at times. She has been to hell and back and isn't afraid to write about it. She is a bit outspoken, probably too blunt and tends to speak her mind. She refuses to break regardless of what life throws at her. She likes to make people think.

She lives life randomly - fueled by lotsa coffee.

J.V. is not a celebrity. She does not hold a bunch of fancy degrees. She is not famous *(yet)* nor different from anyone who reads her work. She is the woman next door, the chick at the coffee shop, and the one singing in her truck at a traffic light. She is a wife, a stepmother, a sister and a friend. J.V. is simply a woman who has seen both the darkest of days and the brightest moments that life has to offer and who one day decided to write about them.

Often J.V. can be found sitting on the rocky coast of Maine staring out lost in thought at the ocean or wandering around the woods behind the home she shares with her husband and son in Gorham, Maine. She almost always has a coffee in hand and a determined look on her face while randomly contemplating life and all of its lessons.

Made in the USA
Lexington, KY
12 July 2013